Encouraged!

Staying Strong in Desperate Days

PAUL
SCHWANKE

Evangelist Paul Schwanke
www.preachthebible.com

Cover design by Mr. Rick Lopez
www.outreachstudio.com

Special thanks to Pastor Ken Brooks
Special thanks to Kelly Schwanke

ISBN-13:978-1539485834
ISBN-10: 1539485838

Printed in the United States of America

CONTENTS

IT HAD JUST GOTTEN worse. A lot worse.

David was running for his life. On those rare occasions when he had a moment to catch his breath, he must have wondered what he did to deserve all of this. The reward for behaving "wisely" was the jealous anger of King Saul, so David spent his nights and days fleeing the sword. From Ramah to Gath to Adullum to Keilah to Ziph to Engedi to Ziph to Gath to Ziklag to Aphek, David fled some 177 miles in panic, looking over his shoulder every step of the way. Three thousand sharpshooters were after him like a hunter goes after a bird. All of his plots and schemes had fallen apart, and even those moments where David exhibited heavenly grace seemed to have been for naught.

Yet, David never imagined the catastrophe he was about to witness.

The stench of the smoke filled their nostrils long before they witnessed the devastation. Little did David know that while he and his men were on their mission to Gath, Amalekite warriors had invaded their city, burned it to the ground, and taken their families captive.[1] When the stunned followers of David saw the smoldering ruins of their home town, they "lifted up their voice and wept, until they had no more power to weep" (1 Samuel 30:4). Their "weeping" was not silent sobbing, but rather a panic-stricken wailing.

Soon the sorrowful men became grieved, bitter men, and they talked of stoning David. As stoning was a form of execution reserved for the most serious of crimes, it is clear how the men of David viewed their leader now.

As for David, he also struggled within and without. Internally, he also feared for his two wives, Ahinoam and Abigail. Externally, the dam holding back the seething anger of his comrades was about to burst. Worse, he did not have a plan. Little wonder then that the Bible says he was "greatly distressed" (1 Samuel 30:5).

The Old Testament word "distressed" is a desperate word. It was normally used to describe that which is narrow, confining, or restricted. At times, the word meant to tie or bind up, such as binding a stone in a sling. On an emotional level, the word pictures a person who is under tremendous pressure and oppression. There is no place to turn with the enemy advancing from all sides.[2]

No place to go. No one to turn to. David was being crushed from within and without. Worse than the impending mutiny of his furious soldiers was the fact that David knew in his heart that he was responsible. His trouble began the day he followed his fears and not his God. Before long, he was telling one falsehood after another until he did the unimaginable crime of yoking with the enemies of Israel. He had brought this on himself.

So David, what are you going to do with your world falling apart? What do you do when you are friendless, forlorn, and forsaken? What happens now that you are "greatly distressed?"

"David encouraged himself in the LORD his God."

Chapter One

Encouragement!

"DAVID ENCOURAGED HIMSELF in the LORD his God."

It is a powerful statement on so many levels. With so much adversity, one would think that David would not have the time for such shallowness. Where had the Amalekites taken their families? How would he sustain his armies? What would he do about the insurrection brewing in the ranks? Every passing moment meant greater risk for the impending danger the women and children faced in enemy hands.

But David *"encouraged himself in the LORD."*

We live in a discouraged world. 77% of the American people regularly deal with physical symptoms caused by stress. In order, the greatest causes are: job pressures; money problems; health problems; relationship problems; poor nutrition; media overload(!); lack of sleep.[3] We are caught in a death spiral of defeatism from which there seems to be no stopping.

Even pastors are discouraged. 90% said they were regularly fatigued and worn out; 71% said they battled depression on a weekly basis; 75% said they were inadequate for the job. No wonder then that 80% of pastors entering the ministry this year will be doing something else within five years.[4]

Discouraged people often cannot sleep at night. When they are awake, they are frequently beset with fear, worry, and restlessness. Discouraged people frequently become complacent people - they simply don't care. In extreme circumstances, discouragement can be a root cause of suicide.

Maybe David was on to something.

So David, help us out. How did you react when the enemy "carried *them* away?" What did you do after you wept until there was "no more power to weep?" How do you live when you are "greatly distressed?"

How did you "encourage" yourself?

It is the reason 1 Samuel 30 is in the Bible. There we can find powerful lessons to help us stay encouraged in this evil day.

We need to understand what encouragement means.

The Old Testament word for "encourage" means to be strong; to be courageous; and to overpower.[5] A form of the word was used to describe a city fortifying its walls and defenses.[6] It was frequently used on the battlefield to admonish a soldier to be strong in combat.[7]

It is the theme of this classic verse:

*"Have not I commanded thee? Be strong and of a good courage;
be not afraid, neither be thou dismayed: for the LORD thy God is
with thee whithersoever thou goest"* (Joshua 1:9).

Notice that encouragement does not mean to be happy.
Though we frequently equate the two, the Bible certainly
does not. There was nothing for David to be happy about
in 1 Samuel 30, but he could be encouraged. It is ridiculous
to think that David was cheerful when he saw that his city
burned to the ground, but he was encouraged. He was not
elated to learn that his wives were gone, but he was
encouraged. He was none too pleased when his brothers
murmured against him, but he was encouraged.

Encouragement and happiness are not the same thing!

There is a lot of money in making people happy. Drug
makers know it. Hollywood knows it. Politicians know it.
And 'big business' religion knows it.

The goal of the Sunday morning gathering is putting a
smile on a face. 'Happy' music and programs have
replaced Bible preaching. Convicting portions of Scripture
are conveniently ignored. Most attendees at houses of
religion know "I can do all things through
Christ" (Philippians 4:13), but very few know "I am
crucified with Christ" (Galatians 2:20). Most know "my
God shall supply all your need" (Philippians 4:19), but
very few know "for to me to live *is* Christ" (Philippians
1:21).

'Big business' religion draws thousands to massive
conferences. In 2014, Yankee Stadium was sold out when
more than 50,000 people filled the ballpark for a night of

"encouragement" with Joel Osteen. Scalpers were reselling tickets to the event for up to $850.[8] At $15 per ticket, plus sales of books and souvenirs, one night at the ole' ballpark rang the coffers for millions of dollars.

There is a lot of money in 'happy.' But 'happy' and 'encouraged' are not the same thing.

God does not expect us to be happy at the funeral of a loved one, but He wants us to be encouraged. God does not expect us to be happy when we lose our job, but He wants us to be encouraged. God does not expect us to be happy when the doctor says, "Cancer," but He wants us to be encouraged.

A frivolous song, a flighty sermon, and a feeble story might paint a fleeting smile on a man's face, but God's solutions are permanent. David didn't need a good feeling, he needed to be as strong as a rock. With his world crumbling on every side, he didn't need a God who would make him healthy, happy, and rich.

He needed to be *"encouraged in the LORD."*

We need to understand that encouragement is a choice.
"David encouraged **himself**."

As circumstances sped out of control, David recognized that his friends were rapidly failing him. He was losing his leadership over the band of 600 warriors, and his alliances with men like King Achish were worthless. There seemed to be nobody to pat him on the back or to tell him to 'press on.' There was no one to share the load.

So he simply encouraged "himself."

Perhaps it sounded like this: "I may not have a friend in the world. This may well be my last day on this earth. I may well lose absolutely everything, but I refuse to be discouraged! I will not let my present circumstances make me a weak and frail man."

It sounds so simplistic and basic. We are almost offended at the notion that a human being can actually make choices that influence his outlook toward life. Since we have been trained to think that all of our problems are the fault of others, we are conditioned to look to external sources for the fixing of those issues.

The doctor can heal me with a prescription. The government can sustain me with an entitlement. A college degree will fix all my financial woes. The more we blame society for our difficulties, the more we expect society to fix the mess it made.

At the end of his rope, David discovered no one remained to encourage him. With comrades ready to stone him, he looked in the mirror, and said, "I choose to be strong. I choose to be courageous. I choose to be encouraged."

It works today. Instead of expecting a magic potion from Walgreens, we need to take matters into our own hands. Instead of looking to artificial escapism from Hollywood, we need to face our own reality. Instead of a paying a psychologist to blame the rest of the world for our personal meltdowns, we need to take responsibility for our own condition.

If David could encourage himself in the throes of the Amalekite calamity, we can encourage ourselves in these "perilous times" (2 Timothy 3:1).

We need to realize that the LORD is our only hope of encouragement.

David recognized his need for strength, and he knew that encouragement was a choice. So how did he accomplish this? It is important to note what did not work.

He did not expect God to automatically snap His fingers and fix the problems. One preacher put it like this:

It is not a quick fix. It is not recognizing that the pressure is on and so deciding to seek help in religion. The Lord is not a genie you rub in trouble in order to make you feel better. Jesus is not your own personal pain reliever to get you on top of life's aches.[9]

David did not conclude that he could solve his problems by venting. Perhaps they tried that in verse four, but the lifting up of voices and weeping fixed nothing.

Nor was the problem resolved by assigning blame. David's men gave that a try in verse 6, but it got them nowhere.

David decided to go to the Lord. Using the priest's ephod, he obeyed the Old Testament pattern for seeking the Will of God.[10] "David enquired at the LORD, saying, Shall I pursue after this troop? shall I overtake them? And he answered him, Pursue: for thou shalt surely overtake *them*, and without fail recover *all*" (1 Samuel 30:8). His troubles came by following his own will; his encouragement came by following God's will.

We have a distinct advantage over David. We no longer pull colored stones out of priestly pouches to determine the Will of God.[11] Instead, we simply open our Bibles where we discover a "more sure word of prophecy" (2 Peter 1:19). The best way to know the Will of God is to be a faithful student of the Word of God.

During the tumultuous days of World War II, America anxiously waited to hear reports from distant battlefields where sons and husbands were dying for freedom. The strain in that hour was extraordinary. In the midst of the war, a Pennsylvania mother named Ruth Caye Jones was reading a Pittsburgh newspaper which listed wartime casualties.

Mrs. Jones put her paper aside and opened her Bible. When she read the words "perilous times shall come," she began to write verses in her notebook. When she stopped writing, the old clock on the mantle chimed four notes prompting her to write music that matched the words. When she was finished, she had a song for the ages:

In times likes these you need a Savior;
In times like these you need an anchor;
Be very sure, be very sure your anchor holds
And grips the Solid Rock!

In times like these you need the Bible;
In times like these O be not idle;
Be very sure, be very sure your anchor holds
And grips the Solid Rock!

In times like these I have a Savior;
In times like these I have an anchor;
I'm very sure, I'm very sure my anchor hold
And grips the Solid Rock!

This Rock is Jesus, yes, He's the One;
This Rock is Jesus, the only One!
Be very sure, be very sure your anchor holds
And grips the Solid Rock![12]

Ruth Caye Jones and David had much in common. They both lived in times that were greatly distressing, yet they each made the choice to run to the "Solid Rock." In so doing, they left us with hope for our present day.

It is how we *encourage ourselves in the Lord.*

Chapter Two
David's Songbook

ARTHUR LUTHER had never felt so helpless. While playing the piano for the O. E. Williams Evangelistic Team in a remote mountain village in Kentucky, he received word over the telegraph line that his little boy had become seriously ill. Six hundred miles separated dad from son, and there was no easy way to get home.

"When I received that word, my world seemed to stop, for I felt so helpless. There I was, so many miles away from home, and in a place where I would either have to walk the many dangerous miles down the mountain, or wait some four or five days before the train could take me out. At that moment, I realized how limited man can be in the extremities of life. In the little Kentucky home where I was staying, I began to collect my thoughts and talk to the Lord, for I knew He alone had the answer to my dilemma."

As Arthur sat at the piano, a simple melody developed under his fingers which seemed to say, "Jesus never fails." Soon the phrase became a chorus, and before the afternoon ended, an entire song was written. Arthur Luther took this little song as an answer to his prayer, and sure enough, a knock came at the door with word that his boy would survive.

Arthur Luther had attempted to write many popular songs yet all had failed. But the one song that God gave him in the hour of need would travel the world encouraging saints to trust their Savior and reminding the lost of hope in a hopeless world.

Earthly friends may prove untrue, doubts and fears assail,
One still loves and cares for you, one who will not fail.

Tho the sky be dark and drear, fierce and strong the gale,
Just remember he is near, and he will not fail.

In life's dark and bitter hour, love will still prevail,
Trust his everlasting power, Jesus will not fail.

Jesus never fails! Jesus never fails!
Heaven and earth may pass away, but Jesus never fails![13]

While sitting at an old square piano in Kentucky, Arthur Luther *encouraged himself in the Lord.* Perhaps he did not realize it at the time, but he was following the footsteps of David. In his darkest hours, God gave him glorious songs. which are recorded for all of eternity in the Bible.[14]

Of the one hundred and fifty Psalms in our Bible, at least seventy four of them have been attributed to David as being the human author.[15] Most of those songs come without a 'superscript' leaving us without a sure knowledge as to the timeframe in David's life when the words were written. However, on numerous occasions, the incident leading to the writing of the Psalm is inserted in the title. These insights provide us with a rich opportunity to understand the circumstances David was facing as God encouraged him with a song.

These Psalms have led to this book. I have attempted to place them in a chronological order of the timeline of David's life. We can almost hear him singing as God delivers him again and again. Slowly, but surely, we watch him grow "in grace, and *in* the knowledge of our Lord and Saviour" (2 Peter 3:18). We are reminded that God does not fail His children in life's darkest hours, and in those difficult times, we can take our Bible and sing the praises of our King.

It is how we *encourage ourselves in the Lord.*

Chapter Three

David on the Run

PSALM 56

To the chief Musician upon Jonathelemrechokim, Michtam of David, when the Philistines took him in Gath.

¹ Be merciful unto me, O God: for man would swallow me up; he fighting daily oppresseth me. ² Mine enemies would daily swallow me up: for they be many that fight against me, O thou most High. ³ What time I am afraid, I will trust in thee. ⁴ In God I will praise his word, in God I have put my trust; I will not fear what flesh can do unto me. ⁵ Every day they wrest my words: all their thoughts are against me for evil. ⁶ They gather themselves together, they hide themselves, they mark my steps, when they wait for my soul. ⁷ Shall they escape by iniquity? in thine anger cast down the people, O God.

⁸ Thou tellest my wanderings: put thou my tears into thy bottle: are they not in thy book? ⁹ When I cry unto thee, then shall mine enemies turn back: this I know; for God is for me. ¹⁰ In God will I praise his word: in the LORD will I praise his word. ¹¹ In God have I put my trust: I will not be afraid what man can do unto me. ¹² Thy vows are upon me, O God: I will render praises unto thee. [13] *For thou hast delivered my soul from death: wilt not thou deliver my feet from falling, that I may walk before God in the light of the living?*

To say the least, it was not David's finest hour.

From the moment the prophet "Samuel took the horn of oil, and anointed him in the midst of his brethren" (1 Samuel 16:13), life had become a whirlwind for David. In the Valley of Elah, David conquered the mighty giant, Goliath of Gath. There was a new friendship with Jonathan and the promotion from King Saul himself. All was fine until the ladies began to sing, "Saul hath slain his thousands, and David his ten thousands" (1 Samuel 18:7). The jealous and fearful monarch could not allow such divided loyalty, so he tried to murder David on two occasions, sent him to fight the Philistines with enormous odds stacked against him, attempted to murder him the third time, and organized a series of manhunts where David was 'public enemy #1.'

Yet, David responded with sterling righteousness. The Bible tells us on no fewer than four occasions that he reacted to Saul's venom "wisely." What a testimony! Saul was consumed by hatred while David was consumed by holiness. Saul was full of fear while David was full of faith. The contradictions were so blatant, Saul's own son sided with David against his father.

David's story is the textbook example of trusting the Lord in the midst of turmoil; of demonstrating grace when surrounded by rage; of resting in God when facing injustice. He was quite the example.

But suddenly, everything changed. It was almost as if someone flipped a switch. David goes from being the prototype of righteousness to being a paradigm of faithlessness. When we read the account of 1 Samuel 21, we can only wonder, "Where did that come from?"

That is the question we always ask when we make a mess of things. Our human experience all too often teaches us that we can walk with God for a long time, make godly decisions, gain a series of victories, and then without warning, create a spiritual disaster. We have all learned the truth of 1 Corinthians 10:12 the hard way: "Wherefore let him that thinketh he standeth take heed lest he fall."

David ran for his life to Ahimelech, the priest of Nob. The events that follow would mold David far more than a first impression might give. In fact, the incidents described in 1 Samuel 21-24 led to the writing of no fewer than seven Psalms.[16] David would sing about these days for the rest of his life. He would not allow himself to forget the lessons he learned.

Ahimelech was alarmed at meeting the hero of Israel. When asked why he had come alone, David managed to tell the priest four lies in one sentence. Convinced that David was on a top secret mission for the government, the man of God gave him food and the sword of Goliath.

The next stop defied logic. One would tend to think that the last place on earth that David would visit would be Goliath's hometown, Gath. However, that is precisely where he went. Soon, he is once again 'public enemy #1,' and the king of Gath, Achish, is ready to kill him.

David's decision-making certainly took a strange turn. His choice to run to Gath and the ensuing path was erratic to say the least, and desperate at the worst. From behaving wisely to behaving foolishly, David in 1 Samuel serves as a reminder of how quickly anyone of us can fall. It begs the question: What happened to David?

We find the answer not once but twice:

"And David arose, and fled that day for fear of Saul, and went to Achish the king of Gath." (1 Samuel 21:10)

"And David laid up these words in his heart, and was sore afraid of Achish the king of Gath." (1 Samuel 21:12)

David was scared to death. His fear led to a series of bad decisions.

A man afraid of spiders once spotted one in the laundry room of his West Seattle home. In order to get rid of it, he grabbed a lighter and a can of spray paint. There is no report about the fate of the spider, but the house caught fire, causing about $60,000 worth of damage. That is a lot of expense to get rid of one spider.[17]

Like David and the gentleman in Seattle, our fears lead to dangerous choices. Whether those fears are legitimate or imaginary, the results are certainly real. Fear has a huge price tag.

So David, help us out. What do we do when "they be many that fight against me?" Where do we turn when the foe "would daily swallow me up?" How do we keep ourselves from being overcome with panic when the enemy is waiting "for my soul?"

How do we *encourage ourselves in the Lord* when we are "afraid?"

It is the reason Psalm 56 is in the Bible. *"What time I am afraid, I will trust in thee."*

Frightened people often speak erratically. Their disjointed sentences represent the panic in their thinking. David gives a series of staccato statements that join together to paint a picture of the turmoil in his mind:

"...man would swallow me up; he fighting daily oppresseth me. Mine enemies would daily swallow me up: for they be many that fight against me...every day they wrest my words: all their thoughts are against me for evil...they gather themselves together, they hide themselves, they mark my steps, when they wait for my soul."

His fear caused him to give too much credit to his enemies. He described them as mere mortals[18], yet he convinced himself that they were able to swallow him up and destroy his "soul." Our fearful minds often tell us that Satan is able to do things to us which have been limited by God. He is not able to swallow up the soul of the child of God, nor is he able to touch one of His children without permission.

His fear wore him down. He was convinced the enemy was *fighting daily*, a Bible way of saying "all day long."[19] He repeats his angst by claiming they were *daily* seeking a way to swallow him up. They were speaking against him *every day*. Every day, the enemy would "wrest...plot...watch...wait." When fear rules our lives, we live in a state of panic which becomes the controlling force that dominates every thought and every action.

His fear turned him into a self-centered man. In the first six verses of Psalm 56, David uses seventeen personal pronouns. In the final six verses of Psalm 56, he refers to God seventeen times. It is not surprising that the first six verses describe David's despair, while the final six verses describe his victory. When our eyes are on ourselves, we will be discouraged by our human frailty. When our eyes are on our God, we will be impressed by His powerful provision.

How encouraging is the final verse of this song! With his enemies multiplying like dark clouds on a western horizon, David testified that God delivered him from "death." That gave him the confidence that his Savior would also deliver his "feet from falling." The Old Testament word "delivered" meant that God rescued him; He snatched him out of harm.[20] A falling David needed God to catch him and place his feet on a solid rock where he could walk before the light of God's face. Walking in the light meant walking in the safe places. In David's day, it also meant walking in happy places.[21]

Nearly a millennia later, the Lord Jesus would refer to David's lesson: "Then spake Jesus again unto them, saying, I am the light of the world: he that followeth me shall not walk in darkness, but shall have the light of life" (John 8:12). It is a bright day when a man's life is rescued. It is a bright day when a man's fears are gone. But it is a far brighter day when a man is saved for eternity.

He went from darkness to light! David has some lessons we need to grasp:

Victory over Fear and our Choice

There are nine occasions in Psalm 56 where David says, "I will," or "I have put." It is impossible to miss David's responsibility here. God's deliverance was freely available, but it was incumbent on David to access His help. There would be no victory until David made his decisions.

Perhaps some people do not actually want victory over fear. We are all prone to pity parties where we obsess over our needs. The pride of our heart deceives us (Obadiah 3). We love to dwell on our favorite topic - me.

It takes conviction and strength to join David in saying, "*I will.*" Instead of dwelling on my situation, "*I will* trust in thee." Instead of endlessly talking, "*I will* praise his word." Instead of fretting over the enemies prowess, "*I will* not fear what flesh can do unto me." Instead of singing my own praises, "*I will* render praises unto thee." There is a concrete decision to be made. Victory begins when we determine to make right choices.

Victory over Fear and our Trust

David's self-confidence led to his present disaster. By following his own thinking, he had endangered the priest of Nob, ruined his personal testimony, and risked his life by traveling to Philistine territory. He certainly learned the hard way: "He that trusteth in his own heart is a fool" (Proverbs 28:26).

In trouble, David places his "trust" in the Lord. In fact, the song gets back to this theme three times:

"What time I am afraid, I will trust in thee." (Verse 3)
"In God I have put my trust." (Verse 4)
"In God have I put my trust." (Verse 11)

In placing his trust in God, David was expressing his confidence that God alone could keep him safe and secure. He was relying solely on the Lord in the hour of turmoil. We normally think of the word "trust" as being similar to the word 'believe,' yet in the language of the Old Testament, there was a significant difference. One would 'believe' on the Lord in the matter of salvation. One would 'trust' the Lord in matters of peace and security.[22] David could trust God to save his soul, and David could trust God to keep him safe in Gath.

The day we believed on the Lord Jesus was a great day. He washed our sins away. He saved our souls for eternity. He made us His children. There are so many wonderful results that stem from the day we trusted Him with our souls.

If we can trust Him with our souls, can we not then trust Him with our daily lives? If we can trust Him for eternity, can we not trust Him for today? When our fear consumes us, we are actually saying to our Savior: "I can trust you to save me from Hell, but I cannot trust you to keep me safe through this problem."

How ridiculous! The One who conquered death and Hell and Satan is more than able to deliver us in our hour of fear!

The African Missionary, David Livingstone, once found himself overcome by fear. In a dangerous region of the world, with his very life at risk, he took his journal and wrote these words:

January 14, 1856

Felt much turmoil of spirit in prospect of having all my plans for the welfare of this great region and this teeming population knocked on the head by savages tomorrow. But I read that Jesus said: All power is given unto Me in heaven and in earth. Go ye therefore and teach all nations, and lo I Am with you alway, even unto the end of the world.' I will not cross furtively tonight as I intended. Should such a man as I flee? Nay verily, I shall take observations for latitude and longitude tonight though they be the last. I feel quite calm now, thank God." [23]

Victory over Fear and the Bible

On three occasions in this brief psalm, David reminds himself to stay close to the Bible. "In God I will praise his word."

David's Bible consisted of the first five books of the Old Testament and possibly Joshua and Judges. He also had the benefit of prophets like Samuel and Nathan declaring God's revelation to him. That was more than enough for David to know where to turn in his hour of need.

How much greater is our opportunity! We have the complete sixty-six books of God's revelation. We have one hundred and fifty psalms to sing. We have life examples of men and women throughout the ages of time. We have the wisdom of the Proverbs. We have the preaching of the prophets. We have the history of God's beloved Israel. We have the glorious life of Christ. We have the construction of His local church. We have multitudes of prophecies that have been fulfilled and will be fulfilled.

"We have also a more sure word of prophecy; whereunto ye do well that ye take heed." (2 Peter 1:19)

The antidote to fear is the Word of God. How we need to remove the Bible from the shelf and let its mighty words calm our anxious souls. The more we wade through the book, the more we know His calming presence in our lives. Before long, we will discover, like David, that we cannot say it enough:

"In God I will praise his word!"

Victory over Fear and a Promise

"God *is* for me."

The four words at the end of verse nine made all the difference to David. There were a lot of enemies against him. King Saul was after him. The many soldiers and staff were after him. The king of Gath and its citizens were after him.

But there was someone on David's side. "God *is* for me." Centuries later, the Apostle Paul would echo these words and cry, "What shall we then say to these things? If God *be* for us, who *can be* against us?" (Romans 8:31) Elisha told his fear stricken servant: "Fear not: for they that *be* with us *are* more than they that *be* with them" (2 Kings 6:16).

Our pagan world is offended by the notion that God takes sides. Worse, the Satanic religion, Islam, has boasted of their murderous acts and assorted atrocities in the name of the false god, allah. To many, the concept of God taking sides is frightening.

The Bible tells a different story:

"Them that honour me I will honour" (1 Samuel 2:30).
"The LORD of hosts is with us; the God of Jacob is our refuge" (Psalm 46:11).
"The LORD is on my side; I will not fear: what can man do unto me?" (Psalm 118:6)
"But the LORD is with me as a mighty terrible one: therefore my persecutors shall stumble, and they shall not prevail: they shall be greatly ashamed; for they shall not prosper: their everlasting confusion shall never be forgotten" (Jeremiah 20:11).

Psalm 56 tells the story of a man on the run who realized that God is for him. God is for David's safety. God is for David's victory. God is for David's strength.

If we will live for him, we will discover that God is for us as well.

He is for the man that trusts in Him (verse 3).
He is for the man that praises His word (verse 4).
He is for the man who believes that God will judge the wicked (verse 7).

He is for the man who believes that God keeps records (verse 8).
He is for the man who believes that God vindicates (verse 9).
He is for the man who exalts the Bible (verse 10).
He is for the man who keeps his vows (verse 12).
He is for the man who walks before God (verse 13).

God is for us!

Little wonder then that David could say, "Thou tellest my wanderings: put thou my tears into thy bottle: *are they not in thy book?*"

"Tellest" is an Old English word that is a mathematical term. Like a bank teller counting money all day, God is numbering each time we wander through the instability of life. That God would count each and every restless wave of our life is a Bible way of expressing God's particular attention to our burdens.[24] Our mundane lives are never too wearisome for Him.

Even better, David said that God put his tears "into thy bottle." An Old Testament bottle was made of an animal skin and prepared in a way so that it would not leak. In the deserts of ancient Israel, liquid was most precious. Water, milk, and juice would be carefully poured into a bottle which contained a very small opening that prevented evaporation. Every single drop mattered.

The picture is beautiful. Every single tear that David shed was carefully collected and preserved by God,[25] and then placed in a bottle that is owned by God ("thy bottle"). Then God kept a permanent record of those tears in his book. The tears that rolled down the cheeks of the fearful fugitive would never be lost or forgotten.

So David reasoned, "I will not be afraid what man can do unto me." Why should he allow fear to dominate his life? "He knoweth the way that I take" (Job 23:10).

When fears dominate our minds, we would do well to sit with David and ponder our Savior's compassion. "Casting all your care upon him; for he careth for you" (1 Peter 5:7). He knows every single burden. He understands every single fear. He knows every worry, every anxiety, and every sleepless night. "What time I am afraid, I will trust in thee."

Years ago, Pastor Frank Graeff was known in his city of Philadelphia as the 'Sunshine Minister.' It was a wonderful reputation to have, but for a great period of time, he actually lived in "despair and defeat." One day, at a place where he felt that he could no longer take it, he dropped to his knees and poured out his heart to the One who cares. Instantly, the peace of God flooded his soul, replacing the raging fear. He cried, "I know He cares! I know my Savior cares!" [26]

Soon the sunshine preacher had a pen in hand and wrote the words that have blessed multitudes of weary hearts since:

Does Jesus care when my heart is pained
Too deeply for mirth and song,
As the burdens press, and the cares distress,
And the way grows weary and long?

Does Jesus care when my way is dark
With a nameless dread and fear?
As the daylight fades into deep night shades,
Does He care enough to be near?

Does Jesus care when I've tried and failed
To resist some temptation strong?
When for my deep grief, I find no relief,
Tho my tears flow all the night long?

Does Jesus care when I've said good-bye
To the dearest on earth to me,
And my sad heart aches, till it nearly breaks,
Is it aught to Him? Does He see?

O yes, He cares! I know He cares!
His heart is touched with my grief;
When the days are weary, the long nights dreary,
I know my Savior cares.[27]

So the sweet psalmist of Israel puts the finishing touches on yet one more inspired song. Off to the choir director it goes to join the collection of the Michtam psalms, hymns as precious as gold. But this time, David supplied not only the lyrics of the cantata, he provided the tune. It was to be sung to the tune called "Jonathelemrechokim," meaning "the silent dove in a distant place."[28] It is the perfect score for the perfect song, for it is the song where God took David from persecution to praise; from battle to boldness; from calamity to confidence. When God is finished with David, he is as tranquil as a gentle dove perched on a branch of a mighty oak tree.

"What time I am afraid, I will trust in thee."

It is how we *encourage ourselves in the Lord.*

Chapter Four
Embarrassed!

PSALM 34

A Psalm of David, when he changed his behaviour before Abimelech; who drove him away, and he departed.

¹ I will bless the LORD at all times: his praise shall continually be in my mouth. ² My soul shall make her boast in the LORD: the humble shall hear thereof, and be glad. ³ O magnify the LORD with me, and let us exalt his name together. ⁴ I sought the LORD, and he heard me, and delivered me from all my fears. ⁵ They looked unto him, and were lightened: and their faces were not ashamed. ⁶ This poor man cried, and the LORD heard him, and saved him out of all his troubles. ⁷ The angel of the LORD encampeth round about them that fear him, and delivereth them. ⁸ O taste and see that the LORD is good: blessed is the man that trusteth in him. ⁹ O fear the LORD, ye his saints: for there is no want to them that fear him. ¹⁰ The young lions do lack, and suffer hunger: but they that seek the LORD shall not want any good thing.

¹¹ Come, ye children, hearken unto me: I will teach you the fear of the LORD. ¹² What man is he that desireth life, and loveth many days, that

he may see good? [13] Keep thy tongue from evil, and thy lips from speaking guile. [14] Depart from evil, and do good; seek peace, and pursue it. [15] The eyes of the LORD are upon the righteous, and his ears are open unto their cry. [16] The face of the LORD is against them that do evil, to cut off the remembrance of them from the earth. [17] The righteous cry, and the LORD heareth, and delivereth them out of all their troubles. [18] The LORD is nigh unto them that are of a broken heart; and saveth such as be of a contrite spirit. [19] Many are the afflictions of the righteous: but the LORD delivereth him out of them all. [20] He keepeth all his bones: not one of them is broken. [21] Evil shall slay the wicked: and they that hate the righteous shall be desolate. [22] The LORD redeemeth the soul of his servants: and none of them that trust in him shall be desolate.

David's fear created a firestorm. A series of bad decisions brought him to the land of Gath where King Achish wanted his head.[29] Then the story goes from strange to bizarre:

"And David laid up these words in his heart, and was sore afraid of Achish the king of Gath. And he changed his behaviour before them, and feigned himself mad in their hands, and scrabbled on the doors of the gate, and let his spittle fall down upon his beard." (1 Samuel 21:12-13)

Achish responded, "Lo, ye see the man is mad: wherefore *then* have ye brought him to me? Have I need of mad men, that ye have brought this *fellow* to play the mad man in my presence? shall this *fellow* come into my house?" (1 Samuel 21:14-15)

In one chapter, David managed to go from champion to cheater, and from military hero to madman. It is a poignant reminder that anyone of us can fall a very long way in a very short time. When he ran out of priests and sanctuaries, he escaped to a cave called Adullam, where his family and friends joined him. "And every one *that was* in distress, and every one that *was* in debt, and every one *that was* discontented, gathered themselves unto him; and he became a captain over them: and there were with him about four hundred men" (1 Samuel 22:2). (Contrary to popular opinion, this is *not* the first Baptist Church in recorded history.)

David would frequent this cave on more than one occasion. Like Moses before him and Elijah after him, there were many lessons God taught David in a cave. It was a place to stop and think, and as he reviewed the recent events in his life, David could only shake his head in embarrassment. He had managed to make a fool of himself. But before long, the walls of that cave were ringing with a new song God had given him. With that song, a shamed man would encourage himself in the Lord.

So David, help us out. When we have embarrassed ourselves, what does "this poor man do?" How do we go on when we are "sore afraid?" What do we do when we have made ourselves look like the "mad" man?

It is the reason Psalm 34 is in the Bible.

Instead of wallowing in self-pity, David sang a mighty hymn exalting God (verses 1-10). Then in verse 11, he gathers children so that he might teach them "the fear of the LORD."

A song and a sermon! Instead of focusing on his shame, David centered his attention back on his Savior. He got in trouble in the first place because he took his eyes off of Jesus. He is not going to compound the problem by keeping his eyes on himself.

So David, what kind of song do you sing when you are shamed? And what kind of lessons did you learn from the fiasco?

The Song (Psalm 34:1-10)

"I will bless the LORD at all times: his praise *shall* continually *be* in my mouth."

Amazing! The last thing we feel like doing when we are ashamed is exalting the Lord. After we have defended ourselves, justified ourselves, and plotted our revenge, we don't have the energy left to magnify Him. But "all times" means "all times." "Continually" means "continually." He is worthy of our worship even when we have created a disaster.

David's self-centeredness created this mess, but he would climb out of the cave by using his "soul...(to) make her boast in the LORD." It is one thing to brag about God with our tongue, but when our soul is the home of our boast, it is far more genuine and authentic.

Soon, it started to catch on. David invited the distressed malcontents to join him in magnifying and exalting the One who could deliver from "all...fears." Before long, the entire cave resounded as a four hundred voice choir lifted their voice in song. Instead of looking at their difficulties, their distresses, and their debts, they were looking "unto him!"

Faces filled with dark shame were suddenly "lightened." The people were glowing and beaming, overjoyed at the grace of God.[30] David testified, "This poor man cried, and the LORD heard *him*, and saved him out of all his troubles." The man who had slain the tens of thousands had been reduced to a miserable wretch, but God still hears miserable wretches! That male choir might well have started to sing their version of Amazing Grace:

Amazing grace! How sweet the sound
That saved a wretch like me!
I once was lost, but now am found;
Was blind, but now I see.

Before long, they discovered someone else was camping out in that cave!

"The angel of the LORD encampeth round about them that fear him, and delivereth them." The "angel of the LORD" in the Old Testament usually refers to a human appearance of none other than the Son of God Himself. He did not only join the camp, but He also surrounded them "round about." He took the most dangerous position. He would take the first hit.

David was incredulous. We can hear him say, "I let Him down. I failed Him. I tried this my own way. But in the end, He never let me down. He never failed me."

And he learned some great lessons along the way. He learned yet again that the "LORD *is* good," that "blessed *is* the man *that* trusteth in him," and "they that seek the LORD shall not want any good *thing*."

We can "taste and see" just like David did. Every life experience with the Savior reminds us that He is faithful, good, and generous. He always has and always will "supply all (our) need according to his riches in glory by Christ Jesus" (Philippians 4:19). We can taste it. We can see it. We can believe it.

He still cares for us even when we have managed to humiliate ourselves.

The Sermon (Psalm 34:11-22)

It is time for Sunday School in the Cave Adullum. "Come, ye children, hearken unto me: I will teach you the fear of the LORD." In his thoughts he may well have added, "And did I ever learn the hard way!"

David told them how to how to have a long life of many days full of the goodness of God. That blessing would not come by lying to a priest. It would not come by running to pagan kings. It would not come by pretending to be a madman. A man operating out of fear is a man who is going to keep digging a deeper pit to fall into.

So he stands up in class and tells the boys and girls the lessons he learned from his excursion into Gath:

Watch your tongue.

We know we should not use our tongue for evil, but David took it a step further. He taught them to be sure they did not use their tongue to deceive with guile (fraud, deceit). He could well tell them how he deceived a priest and a king, and his lies snowballed.

"Oh be careful little tongue what you say..."

Watch your steps.

"Depart from evil, and do good." Have you noticed that the government is funding commercials that are teaching people the importance of being nice? Since God has been tossed out of our schools, our government, our courts, and our living rooms, someone has to tell people they should be nice.

It worked a whole lot better when boys and girls would sit in a Sunday School class where a teacher would hold a Bible and tell them to "depart from evil and do good." In the 'old days,' we didn't need playgrounds, video games, and rock concerts, because we believed the Word of God was sufficient.

Perhaps instead of trying to be 'culturally relevant,' churches ought to try having a teacher tell the students that God wants them to "depart from evil, and do good."

"Oh be careful little feet where you go..."

Be a peacemaker.

David told the boys and girls, "seek peace, and pursue it." "As much as lieth in you, live peaceably with all men" (Romans 12:18). A few days earlier, he was frothing at the mouth and on the verge of starting a war. Now, he is telling boys and girls there is something more important than conquering Goliaths. God wants his children to chase after peace.

The he reminded them, "The eyes of the LORD *are* upon the righteous, and his ears *are open* unto their cry." Notice that both eyes of the LORD and both ears of the LORD are upon the righteous man. He is watching and He is listening with full attention.

"For the Father up above is looking down in tender love..."

What a tremendous lesson! When we have embarrassed ourselves, we need to follow the steps of David. First, let's lift up our voice in song and magnify the mighty name of God. Then come Sunday morning, let's head over to the Sunday School class and invest our lives in some boys and girls. Before long, our priorities will change because the needs of those little ones are a whole lot more important than our personal problems!

One day, a hospital chaplain named Dyson Hague was visiting a ward of dying soldiers. One man asked him if he would write his Sunday school teacher and tell her he would die a Christian because of her teaching.

Chaplain Hague wrote the letter. A few weeks later he received this reply: "Just a month ago I resigned my class of young men which I had been teaching for years, for I felt that my teaching was getting nowhere. Then came your letter, telling how my teaching had helped win this boy to Christ. I've asked for my class back. May God have mercy on me!"[31]

'Now' is always a good time to praise our God. 'Now' is always a good time to teach boys and girls. It is how we *encourage ourselves in the Lord.*

Chapter Five

When the Bad Guy Wins

PSALM 52

To the chief Musician, Maschil, A Psalm of David, when Doeg the Edomite came and told Saul, and said unto him, David is come to the house of Ahimelech.

¹ Why boastest thou thyself in mischief, O mighty man? the goodness of God endureth continually. ² Thy tongue deviseth mischiefs; like a sharp razor, working deceitfully. ³ Thou lovest evil more than good; and lying rather than to speak righteousness. Selah. ⁴ Thou lovest all devouring words, O thou deceitful tongue. ⁵ God shall likewise destroy thee for ever, he shall take thee away, and pluck thee out of thy dwelling place, and root thee out of the land of the living. Selah.

⁶ The righteous also shall see, and fear, and shall laugh at him: ⁷ Lo, this is the man that made not God his strength; but trusted in the abundance of his riches, and strengthened himself in his wickedness. ⁸ But I am like a green olive tree in the house of God: I trust in the mercy of God for ever and ever. ⁹ I will praise thee for ever, because thou hast done it: and I will wait on thy name; for it is good before thy saints.

It seems like such an innocent statement in the Bible. When David stood in the presence of Ahimelech the priest and asked for bread and a sword, Doeg (pronounced Doe-eeg) was there. Nothing in Doeg's background or present life suggested a desire to worship the God of Israel. When the Bible says he was "detained," it tells us he was forced to be there. As chief of Saul's security, he was on assignment.[32]

Doeg was not spying on David. He was, depending on your viewpoint, either in the right place at the right time or the wrong place at the wrong time. There is plenty of fault to be pinned on Doeg, and subsequent events would demonstrate how evil he truly was. However, there was nothing sinister about his presence at the Tabernacle. It happened by chance that he was present when David arrived.

Therein lies the problem of either racing ahead of God or straggling behind Him. David has to find ways to cover his steps. He has to keep looking over his shoulder to see who might be watching. He has to constantly determine whose side everyone is on. He is acting like a politician.

As David was carrying the sword of Goliath to Philistine territory, Doeg was scurrying over the hills north of Jerusalem and back to the palace. When King Saul was in the middle of a rant accusing his staff of being in league with David, Doeg spoke up: "I saw the son of Jesse coming to Nob, to Ahimelech the son of Ahitub. And he enquired of the LORD for him, and gave him victuals, and gave him the sword of Goliath the Philistine" (1 Samuel 22:9-10).

Ahimelech, his family, and the remaining priests from the village of Nob were arrested and charged with conspiracy. When the man of God defended the character of David, the fate of the whole group was sealed. Saul ordered his footmen to execute the priests. When they refused his direct order, the king turned to Doeg and charged, "Turn thou, and fall upon the priests" (1 Samuel 22:18).

The genocide that followed demonstrated Doeg's bloodthirstiness. On that one day, he murdered eighty-five priests. He then returned to Nob and "smote (them)...with the edge of the sword, both men and women, children and sucklings, and oxen, and asses, and sheep, with the edge of the sword" (1 Samuel 22:19). It was devastating.

One of priest's sons, Abiathar, escaped and fled to David. When he told the report, David took responsibility. "I knew *it* that day, when Doeg the Edomite *was* there, that he would surely tell Saul: I have occasioned *the death* of all the persons of thy father's house" (1 Samuel 22:22). Once again, a bad situation had turned worse.

It would be a long time before Doeg would pay for his crime. In fact, outside of Psalm 52, there is no other reference in the Bible to this event, nor are there any of these verses quoted in the New Testament. The only reference from Jewish historians informs us that he went on to be a "great scholar."[33] Doeg seemed to have dodged the proverbial bullet, at least for as long as he lived on this earth.

So David, help us out. What do we do when evil people "boast...in mischief?" What about the defenseless atrocities heaped upon the "righteous?" How do we respond to the people who trust "in the abundance of his riches," and make themselves strong in "wickedness?"

How do we *encourage ourselves in the Lord* when so many wicked people seem to get away with their crimes?

It is the reason Psalm 52 is in the Bible. There are no dulcet strings playing this song. The chief musician and his choir are singing a maschil-a song used to instruct the people. David wants to inform the Doegs of the world that they have an appointment with a holy God. David wants the righteous man to know that God will get it right. At the conclusion of this number there would be no 'amens' or 'hallelujahs.' Retribution is serious business.

The song begins with the exposing of Doeg's wickedness. We sometimes wonder if God sees how the wicked are behaving, but there is no worry. God saw Doeg as he really was.

Doeg was a "mighty man," a warrior of prowess and exceptional strength, and he knew it. He loved to boast "in mischief." The Hebrew word for 'boast' is a powerful study. It is also translated as 'praise' and is most commonly used in the Bible in exalting God. The root of the word refers to the "giving off of light by celestial bodies."[34] When we praise God, we want all the light and attention to be directed to Him. When Doeg boasted, he wanted all the lights to shine on himself. He had to be the center of attention; the only star in the sky.

His arrogance is magnified by the words "thou thyself." He freely admitted to the horrific act of genocide against the village of Nob, smugly convincing himself that he could not be stopped. He personally confronted the "goodness of God" which *"endureth* continually." It is awfully hard for a human to exhaust the mercy, kindness, faithfulness, loyalty, and love of God, but Doeg managed to accomplish just that.

Doeg's filthy mouth epitomized his dirty soul. His words were like the "sharp razor" a barber used to cut a man's hair. Charles Spurgeon mused that his razor-like tongue may at times been used softly and deftly like an Oriental barber, while on other occasions, that razor may have rapidly sliced a man's throat. "Whetted by malice, and guided by craft, he did his cruel work with accursed thoroughness."[35]

It is one thing for a man to do evil, but Doeg had a passion for it. "Thou lovest evil more than good; *and* lying rather than to speak righteousness...thou lovest all devouring words." A man like Doeg lives to sin. There is no wickedness missing in his playbook. He wakes up in the morning plotting, planning, and conniving. No one can trust him.

A murderer. A bully. A narcissist. A liar. God had his number.

The attendants at Saul's palace and the citizens of Nob trembled before such a man, but God was not afraid of him, nor is He afraid of any terrorist. He delivered four blunt promises directly to Doeg:

"God shall likewise destroy thee for ever, he shall take thee away, and pluck thee out of thy dwelling place, and root thee out of the land of the living."

The promise to destroy Doeg meant that God would pound him into the ground like a building that is razed until nothing is left. God would utterly wipe him out. The phrase "take away" pictures a tree that is torn out of the ground by someone twisting and pulling. As he had ripped Ahimelech out of his home and family, so God would "pluck" him out of his house. When God was finished with Doeg there would not be so much as a root left. God's judgment would be absolute and final.

This side of eternity, it does not always work that way. On this earth, justice is not always just.

On July 14, 2015, the Center for Medical Progress began to release a series of videos depicting horrific crimes against unborn children committed by the pagan 'nonprofit' organization, Planned Parenthood. At least ten videos were viewed by millions of people creating a firestorm of rage.[36] Decent people around the world were shocked at the calloused barbarity of alleged medical professionals.

Enraged American citizens demanded their political leaders respond. Within days, publicity-seeking politicians promised to defund the organization, yet on December 16th, the Republican led Congress not only voted to fully fund Planned Parenthood, they also gave them a $286 million dollar bonus.[37] A month later, a grand jury cleared the organization of any wrongdoing and indicted the two citizens that produced the videos.

It is not easy being encouraged. It would seem a lot easier to throw our hands up in the air and quit. Our world has become so pagan and so profane that the situation seems hopeless. But David found a way to remind us that all is not as destitute as it seems. God will see that the Doegs, the Planned Parenthood crowd, and the dissembling politicians will answer for their depravity. The last trial has not yet started, and the last verdict has not been read.

There is hope in Psalm 52 for the righteous man. One day, God promised that Doeg would get his comeuppance, and when that happened, the "righteous also shall see." The massacred priests would see the tables turned. They would respond with an awesome "fear" of the perfect justice of God and a holy "laugh" at the appropriate sentence meted out. They would point at Doeg and say, "Lo, this is the man that made not God his strength; but trusted in the abundance of his riches, and strengthened himself in his wickedness."

It is the lesson Jesus taught us. His enemies said he was possessed with a devil. They called him a Samaritan, a glutton, a wine-bibber, a blasphemer, a demoniac, one in league with Beelzebub, a perverter of the nation, and a deceiver of the people. He was struck in His face, crowned with thorns, beaten with a reed, scourged, forced to bear His own cross, and crucified. He was more than able to destroy his enemies without breaking a sweat, yet in that hour of injustice, he taught us how to respond:

"Who, when he was reviled, reviled not again; when he suffered, he threatened not; but committed himself to him that judgeth righteously" (1 Peter 2:23).

In the early 1900's, a humble preacher named George Young invested his life in small, rural churches in the American heartland. He and his wife had a deep love for Christ, and the joy they knew serving Him easily overcame any self pity they may have felt for their poverty. When he wasn't preaching, George was a carpenter living hand to mouth.

The Youngs literally saved every dime they could, and when a friend provided a piece of property, they were able to build a little home. When the house was finished, they stood in the doorway singing, "Praise God from whom all blessings flow!" How thankful they were for God's blessing.

Soon it was time to leave home and preach in a little country church. After the meeting, they headed home anticipating the time they would spend in their 'dream' house. Little did they know that while they were away, an enemy of the Gospel had burned their house to the ground. Every keepsake, every photo, and every possession was now a heap of ashes.

When George Young stood in the middle of those ashes, the sweet presence of God filled his heart. Before long, words filled his mind, and they soon would be written down. Those words would serve to remind the saved that God's name is still "good."

In shady, green pastures, so rich and so sweet,
God leads His dear children along;

Where the water's cool flow bathes the weary one's feet,
God leads His dear children along.

Sometimes on the mount where the sun shines so bright,
God leads His dear children along;
Sometimes in the valley, in darkest of night,
God leads His dear children along.

Though sorrows befall us and evils oppose,
God leads His dear children along;
Through grace we can conquer, defeat all our foes,
God leads His dear children along.

Away from the mire, and away from the clay,
God leads His dear children along;
Away up in glory, eternity's day,
God leads His dear children along.

Some through the waters, some through the flood,
Some through the fire, but all through the blood;
Some through great sorrow, but God gives a song,
In the night season and all the day long.[38]

Suddenly, David does not see the swirling disaster of the present day. He realizes that a man living for God is "like a green olive tree." The olive tree was an incredible illustration of blessing. It produced gallons of oil used for food, medicine, ointments, and light.[39] Better yet, the olive tree would survive for hundreds of years. David would outlast Doeg.

So David calls for the choir director and says, "I have a song for the man who has lost hope. I have a song for the victim of unfair oppression. We can 'trust in the mercy of God for ever and ever.' We can 'praise (Him) for ever.' We can 'wait on (His) name.' He is still leading His children along!"

It is how we *encourage ourselves in the Lord.*

Chapter Six

Betrayed!

PSALM 54

To the chief Musician on Neginoth, Maschil, A Psalm of David, when the Ziphims came and said to Saul, Doth not David hide himself with us?

¹ Save me, O God, by thy name, and judge me by thy strength. ² Hear my prayer, O God; give ear to the words of my mouth. ³ For strangers are risen up against me, and oppressors seek after my soul: they have not set God before them. Selah.

⁴ Behold, God is mine helper: the Lord is with them that uphold my soul. ⁵ He shall reward evil unto mine enemies: cut them off in thy truth. ⁶ I will freely sacrifice unto thee: I will praise thy name, O LORD; for it is good. ⁷ For he hath delivered me out of all trouble: and mine eye hath seen his desire upon mine enemies.

Life in Dublin, Ireland, in the early 1800's was certainly promising for young Joseph Scriven. He had finished his college education and was preparing to enter the business world. When his Irish sweetheart said "Yes," they set about the business of planning a Christian family.

The day before their wedding, his fiancé tragically drowned. As a stunned Scriven watched her lifeless body being lifted from the water, he entered a descent into despair that would affect him for years. He moved to Canada in hopes that new scenery would allow him to forget his past heartache, but the burden followed him across the seas.

Ten years later, having received word that his mother was facing a similar season of despair, he wrote a poem entitled *A Friend Who Understands*. The poem was published anonymously and soon became a beloved hymn.

Years later, a nurse caring for an old Joseph Scriven found the original words to the poem. When asked why he did not let anyone know he was the author, he humbly stated that the words were personal between him and his Savior.[40] Those 'private' words have certainly been a glorious comfort and encouragement to countless millions:

What a friend we have in Jesus,
All our sins and griefs to bear!
What a privilege to carry
Everything to God in prayer!
Oh, what peace we often forfeit,
Oh, what needless pain we bear,
All because we do not carry
Everything to God in prayer!

Have we trials and temptations?
Is there trouble anywhere?

We should never be discouraged —
Take it to the Lord in prayer.
Can we find a friend so faithful,
Who will all our sorrows share?
Jesus knows our every weakness;
Take it to the Lord in prayer.

Are we weak and heavy-laden,
Cumbered with a load of care?
Precious Savior, still our refuge —
Take it to the Lord in prayer.
Do thy friends despise, forsake thee?
Take it to the Lord in prayer!
In His arms He'll take and shield thee,
Thou wilt find a solace there.

Sadly, this final verse is often omitted in our hymnbooks:

Blessed Savior, Thou hast promised
Thou wilt all our burdens bear;
May we ever, Lord, be bringing
All to Thee in earnest prayer.
Soon in glory bright, unclouded,
There will be no need for prayer —
Rapture, praise, and endless worship
Will be our sweet portion there.[41]

With the cries of the innocent citizens of Nob still rising to the holy ears of God, the conspiracy against David only intensified. The sword of Doeg dripped with the blood of the people, yet in the midst of the bloodshed, God delivered Abiathar, the son of the lead priest Ahimelech. He ran for his life carrying the sacred ephod, the garment used to determine the will of God.

With God's permission, David and his 600 men defeated the Philistines and rescued the town of Keilah. When King Saul heard where David was hiding, his arrogance deluded him to conclude that "God hath delivered (David) into mine hand." He "called all the people together to war, to go down to Keilah, to besiege David and his men" (1 Samuel 23:7-8). Using the ephod, God showed David that the thankless citizens of Keilah would stab him in the back and deliver him to Saul. So David was on the run again, settling in the wilderness in a place called Ziph. "And Saul sought him every day, but God delivered him not into his hand" (1 Samuel 23:14).

David must have felt a sense of safety with the Ziphims. They were, after all, of the tribe of Judah, just as he was (Joshua 15:55). It was hardly surprising that a despicable butcher like Doeg would betray him, but David could expect different treatment from his brothers. Surely, he could trust them.

But the Ziphims one-upped Doeg. They managed to betray David twice. The first time, they gave Saul very specific instructions as to how to find him: "Doth not David hide himself with us in strong holds in the wood, in the hill of Hachilah, which *is* on the south of Jeshimon?" (1 Samuel 23:19). Later, they would rat him out again: "And the Ziphites came unto Saul to Gibeah, saying, Doth not

David hide himself in the hill of Hachilah, *which is* before Jeshimon?" (1 Samuel 26:1) If that weren't enough, they even invited the king to "come down according to all the desire of thy soul to come down; and our part *shall be* to deliver him into the king's hand" (1 Samuel 23:20).

Betrayed. A woman who has been deserted by her husband would understand where David was. A pastor who has been dismissed by a church of people that he invested his life in would understand where David was. A businessman who has been dumped by a partner would understand where David was.

He was betrayed by his own brothers.

So David, help us out. What do we do "when strangers are risen up against (us)?" How do we go on when "oppressors seek after (our) souls?" Where do we turn when we are at war with those who "have not set God before them?"

How do we *encourage ourselves in the Lord* when we are pulling the knife out of our backs?

It is the reason Psalm 54 is in the Bible. The Ziphims did not drive David to rage. They did not drive David to revenge. They did not drive David to resentment.

They drove David to his knees. And from his knees, David teaches us how to pray when our world is crumbling.

His prayer was simple. "Save me...hear my prayer...give ear to the words of my mouth." These are blunt words from a burdened man, yet they teach us how simple a prayer life must be. David was not trying to impress anyone with his prayer. The simple cry of a child in trouble is all that is needed to move the heart of God.

His prayer was desperate. David's life was in danger, so he called upon God to "save" him. This was not the cry of a lost man trusting God's salvation, it was the plea of a man whose life was in danger. Like a swimmer drowning in the water, or a victim pleading from a top floor of a house afire, David was unable to rescue himself. This crisis would have to be handled by God.

His prayer came from a powerless man. If David were to survive this encounter, it would not be the result of his human abilities. He looked to heaven and recognized his hope was "by thy name, and...by thy strength." By calling upon the name of the Creator, David was inviting His presence and involvement. John Phillips wrote: "A God who can create galaxies is not intimidated by a man like Saul! A God who keeps order over all His creation is not going to let down one who is trusting in Him. If God was with him, then all was well." [42]

His prayer came from a righteous man. He was willing to step into the courtroom and invite a cross examination. "Judge me." David knew that God knew he had done right by the Ziphims. His confidence in the righteousness of God allowed him to believe he would be vindicated and exonerated by the only One who mattered. One cannot pray like this unless he has nothing to hide. Human justices may be deceived, but the judge of "the quick and the dead" will never be fooled.

His prayer was bold. David seems to be demanding: "Hear my prayer, O God; give ear to the words of my mouth." The idea of a lowly peasant demanding an audience with the most honored and highest adjudicator is inconceivable, yet he is not backing down. There is no human who cares enough or is powerful enough to deliver David, so he calls for a hearing from almighty God. Even more stunning is the fact that he gets that audience.

His prayer was vocal. These were the "words of my mouth," indicating that David prayed out loud. While God is well able to discern a silent prayer, the audible cry of a man is a prayer on a different level. When we pray aloud it is easier to stay on track and compose our request. Publicly praying puts us on the record that we are depending upon God to meet the need.

He prayed to a God who takes sides. This is a difficult concept in our present day where nothing is black and white but rather, shades of gray. The world is offended by the audacity of a man or woman who dares to think that God chooses a side, yet He does choose. He chooses to stand with righteous people. It is the reason David could point at the Ziphites and say, "Strangers are risen up against me, and oppressors seek after my soul: they have not set God before them." Though the enemies of David were actually men of Judah, they had long since abandoned God's word and had become spiritual strangers. Instead of protecting their brother, they were the "oppressors (of his) soul." As their father, Judah, betrayed his own brother Joseph, they were willing to abandon David to the hand of backstabbing Saul. It is more than appropriate to point out the hypocrisy and duplicity of wicked men when pleading with God.

He prayed to the God who uses people. Modern scholars are a little miffed at these words: "the Lord is with them that uphold my soul." The thought that God is simply numbered among David's helpers does not meet their approval, so they rewrite their bibles to say; "the Lord is the upholder of my life."[43] They are missing the entire point.

David is rejoicing that God is using human instruments in his hour of crisis. Even in this story, God rescued Abiathar who in turn rescued David. Behind the scenes, God was using David's close friend Jonathan, to spare his life. The God who is able to guide a stone through the air so that it hits the giant's forehead is also the God who can use a friend with just the right encouragement.

He prayed to the God who upholds. The word "uphold" describes the Lord supporting and sustaining David. He was the friend with the arm around David's shoulders helping him stand. He was the companion ready to grab David's arm when he was about to fall. David learned that God is not only able to meet every need, He knows precisely the appropriate remedy for every need.

He prayed to the God who gets it right. Stamped on David's thinking were the brutal atrocities of Doeg. Crushing David's heart was the betrayal of his own people. Still, with complete confidence in God, he could say, "He shall reward evil unto mine enemies: cut them off in thy truth." He believed in what one writer called the 'boomerang effect' of sin: what goes around will surely come around.[44]

If the Jewish historians are accurate, Doeg did not get his payment until he met God, but that was okay with David. That God would pay Doeg back was all that concerned him. When God was ready to deal with the Ziphims, David was certain it would be just. David was willing to allow God to operate on His own schedule.

He prayed with incredible confidence. The Psalm concludes on an amazing note: "For he hath delivered me out of all trouble: and mine eye hath seen *his desire* upon mine enemies." Compare these words with the introduction: "A Psalm of David, when the Ziphims came and said to Saul, Doth not David hide himself with us?" With trouble and betrayal swirling around him, David prayed and thanked God as if the answer had already come. He was so certain that God would meet the need on a perfect timetable that he thanked Him in advance!

How could David be so certain? The answer is in verse 4: "God is mine helper." God had delivered David so many times there was now a track record. His relationship with the Savior left him with no doubt that God would do it again.

And God did it again! The first twenty-six verses of 1 Samuel 23 play out like a comedy. Saul is here and David is there. Saul goes there and David goes here. Saul was on one side of a mountain while David was on the other. Though Saul was relentless in his pursuit, God was even more determined in His protection. "And Saul sought him every day, but God delivered him (David) not into his hand" (1 Samuel 23:14).

When the Lord had enough cat and mouse, He gave Saul something real to worry about. "But there came a messenger unto Saul, saying, Haste thee, and come; for the Philistines have invaded the land. Wherefore Saul returned from pursuing after David, and went against the Philistines" (1 Samuel 23:27-28).

Sure enough. God did it again.

Out comes the scroll and pen, and David has yet another song for the choir director. He is going to tell us what to do when our friends have despised us and forsaken us:

Take it to the Lord in prayer.

It is how we *encourage ourselves in the Lord.*

Chapter Seven

David in the Lions' Den

PSALM 57

To the chief Musician, Altaschith, Michtam of David, when he fled from Saul in the cave.

¹ Be merciful unto me, O God, be merciful unto me: for my soul trusteth in thee: yea, in the shadow of thy wings will I make my refuge, until these calamities be overpast. ² I will cry unto God most high; unto God that performeth all things for me. ³ He shall send from heaven, and save me from the reproach of him that would swallow me up. Selah. God shall send forth his mercy and his truth. ⁴ My soul is among lions: and I lie even among them that are set on fire, even the sons of men, whose teeth are spears and arrows, and their tongue a sharp sword. ⁵ Be thou exalted, O God, above the heavens; let thy glory be above all the earth. ⁶ They have prepared a net for my steps; my soul is bowed down: they have digged a pit before me, into the midst whereof they are fallen themselves. Selah.

⁷ My heart is fixed, O God, my heart is fixed: I will sing and give praise. ⁸ Awake up, my glory; awake, psaltery and harp: I myself will awake early. ⁹ I will praise thee, O Lord, among the people: I will sing unto thee among the nations. ¹⁰ For thy mercy is great unto the heavens, and thy truth unto the clouds. ¹¹ Be thou exalted, O God, above the heavens: let thy glory be above all the earth.

David knew his struggles were far from over. The Lord gave him a desperately needed respite from the angry king, but eventually, Saul would be done with the Philistines, and then he would be back. His top priority, after all, was capturing and killing the renegade Psalmist.

So once again, David found himself in a cave. Earlier, when he fled from King Achish, he fled to the cave Adullum. Now, on the run from Saul, he landed in a cave in the wilderness of Engedi.[45]

David had managed to make a lot of enemies in a rather short timeframe, including the King of the Philistines and the demonic Doeg. Then Saul chased him to Keilah where he once again escaped with his life. He assumed his brothers in Ziph would protect him, but when they sold him out, he fled to the wilderness of Engedi.

"And it came to pass, when Saul was returned from following the Philistines, that it was told him, saying, Behold, David is in the wilderness of Engedi. Then Saul took three thousand chosen men out of all Israel, and went to seek David and his men upon the rocks of the wild goats" (1 Samuel 24:1-2).

No rest for the weary here.

In Psalm 57:4, David described his life condition like this: "My soul is among lions: and I lie even among them that are set on fire, even the sons of men, whose teeth are spears and arrows, and their tongue a sharp sword." Like man-eating lions gliding through the African savannah, his many foes wanted to rip him to shreds. They were ablaze with a passionate fire that could only be quenched by a dead David. What they could not accomplish with a sword, they would happily do with their pernicious fangs:

"As for that busy member the tongue, in the case of the malicious, it is a two edged, keen, cutting, killing sword. The tongue, which is here compared to a sword, has the adjective sharp added to it, which is not used in reference to the teeth, which are compared to spears, as if to show that if men were actually to tear us with their teeth, like wild beasts, they could not thereby wound us so severely as they can do with their tongues. No weapon is so terrible as a tongue sharpened on the devil's grindstone."[46]

It is the classic Bible story of 'David in the Lions' Den.'

It is easy to read these Psalms and think they all sound alike. David was in trouble, so David prayed. God delivered him and David rejoiced. But Psalm 57 has a different message. This song tells us that David was learning his lessons. He was growing "in grace, and *in* the knowledge of our Lord and Saviour Jesus Christ" (2 Peter 3:18). This is not the story of a man on a perpetual roller coaster who is up one day, down the next, only to rise again. It is the story of a man who is learning how to be *encouraged in the Lord.*

In Psalm 56, David is nervous and frightened. His words are as scattered as his thoughts. It is almost as if David is convincing himself to trust the Lord.

In Psalm 57, David is far calmer. As his life story goes, the lessons of Psalm 34, Psalm 52, and Psalm 54 occurred between Psalm 56 and Psalm 57. The months of running, hiding, and worrying did not take the expected spiritual toll on David; instead, they built him. God used the anxieties and despair to make him stronger.

Three thousand of the finest soldiers in the Israeli army followed Saul to find little ole' David. They were as mighty hunters seeking one little 'bird.' "For, lo, the wicked bend *their* bow, they make ready their arrow upon the string, that they may privily shoot at the upright in heart" (Psalm 11:2). David is outmanned, outgunned, and outnumbered. If there ever were a time for panic, this was that time.

But notice the peace and confidence as David responded to the crisis:

"Yea, in the shadow of thy wings will I make my refuge...I will cry unto God...(who) performeth all things for me. He shall send from heaven, and save me from the reproach of him that would swallow me up...God shall send forth his mercy and his truth."

What a glorious picture! God is spreading out his massive, divine wings, and David is hiding in the shadow. It was not the shadow of the Cave of Engedi that sheltered David, but rather, the mighty wingspan of His God. The words "refuge" and "trusteth" in verse one come from the same Hebrew word. David has learned to trust the Lord for his soul and his life.

Under His wings, under His wings,
Who from His love can sever?
Under His wings my soul shall abide,
Safely abide forever.[47]

He did not react quite like that in previous songs. There are many great lessons that God teaches us in crisis that we cannot learn when all is well. We never enjoy those learning sessions, but they are vital if we will "walk worthy of the Lord unto all pleasing, being fruitful in every good work, and increasing in the knowledge of God; Strengthened with all might, according to his glorious power, unto all patience and longsuffering with joyfulness" (Colossians 1:10-11).

So David, help us out. What do we do when we are facing multitudes of 'calamities?' How do we respond to the "net(s)" that wicked people have set in our way to trap us? What do we do when our souls are "bowed down" in distress?

How do we *encourage ourselves in the Lord* when we find ourselves in the lions' den?

It is the reason Psalm 57 is in the Bible. *"In the shadow of thy wings will I make my refuge."*

As it was with David, our 'lions' can take many forms. Perhaps an unsaved spouse or family member is making your life miserable. It may be a coworker on the job criticizing every move that you make. It may be a student or teacher in school who despises the Savior and your willingness to stand for Him. Perhaps as a soldier in the military, you face your 'lions' late at night in the barracks.

There is no shortage of willing combatants ready to follow their father, the Devil, to the battlefield.

A preacher of yesteryear put it like this:

Why did the psalmist call them lions? "Dogs" is about as good a name as they deserve. Why call them lions? Because at times the Christian man is exposed to enemies who are very strong—perhaps strong in the jaw—very strong in biting, rending, and tearing. Sometimes the Christian man is exposed to those who loudly roar out their infidelities and their blasphemies against Christ, and it is an awful thing to be among such lions as those. The lion is not only strong but cruel; and it is real cruelty which subjects well-meaning men to reproach and misrepresentation. The enemies of Christ and his people are often as cruel as lions, and would slay us if the law permitted them. The lion is a creature of great craftiness, creeping along stealthily, and then making a sudden spring; and so will the ungodly creep up to the Christian, and, if possible, spring upon him when they can catch him in an unguarded moment. [48]

Psalm 57 gives some great insight to surviving the lions' den.

First, we must have a fixed heart. We normally think of the heart as the home of our emotions, but to David, the heart encompassed not only his feelings, but also his desires and his will. It was his inner person. When the Bible commanded the Old Testament saint to "love the LORD thy God with all thine heart, and with all thy soul, and with all thy might" (Deuteronomy 6:5), it meant that a man was to love the Lord with his entire essence. To survive the lions' den would involve David's emotions, his desires, his will, his thinking, and his morals.[49]

His entirety would have to be "fixed." In the language of the Old Testament, the word "fixed" was put in the forefront of the sentence to show priority. In addition, when we find a phrase repeated, ("My heart is fixed...my heart is fixed,") it is a literary way of paying great attention. It would sound like this in the language of David: "Fixed is my heart!!!"

A fixed heart is a heart that is firm, established, and prepared. A fixed heart is there for the long term; it is entrenched and is not moving.[50] It is the result of a Christian who spends a lot of time in his Bible building strong conviction. It is the result of commitment and vows that will not bow to the pressure of a pagan culture. It is the result of a child of God whose Father has proven Himself repeatedly, so there is no longer any doubt about His ability to deliver or His promise to keep His word.

Life was certainly difficult in the early 1900's for Thomas Chisholm. Born in a log cabin in Kentucky, he trusted Christ as a young adult and surrendered his days to serve his Savior. Decades later he wrote:

My income has never been large at any time due to impaired health in the earlier years which has followed me on until now. But I must not fail to record here the unfailing faithfulness of a covenant keeping God, and that He has given me many wonderful displays of His providing care which have filled me with astonishing gratefulness.

A life spent walking with God prepared an old Thomas Chisholm to give us this wonderful gift:

Great is Thy faithfulness, O God my Father
There is no shadow of turning with Thee;
Thou changest not, Thy compassions, they fail not:
As Thou hast been Thou forever wilt be.

Great is Thy faithfulness, great is Thy faithfulness
Morning by morning new mercies I see
All I have needed Thy hand hath provided
Great is Thy faithfulness, lord, unto me!

Summer and winter, and springtime and harvest
Sun, moon, and stars in their courses above,
Join with all nature in manifold witness
To Thy great faithfulness, mercy, and love.

Pardon for sin and a peace that endureth,
Thine own dear presence to cheer and to guide,
Strength for today and bright hope for tomorrow
Blessings all mine, with ten thousand beside! [51]

The fixed man learns that God is always faithful. He is not rattled when circumstances appear bleak, nor does he panic when there seems to be no path to victory. His days have taught him the fidelity of his Lord.

In addition to a fixed heart, we must also have an awakened heart. In verse eight, David used the word "awake" three times which again should capture our attention. It is a word of action meaning to be stirred; to be aroused.[52] When David awoke his glory, he wanted to give the best of his life to the Lord. This is a Bible way of saying that God deserved the greatest honor David could humanly deliver. To do so, he would need to stir up the strings of the orchestra and sing from the depths of his soul. It would seem that David woke up early in the morning to accomplish that.

It is great advice for us. Before the day begins with all its activity and busyness, we do well to give our best to the Lord. We give Him our best time to study the Bible, our best time to offer a song of praise, and our best time to pray.

It is disappointing that we often give Him the leftovers. All too often, I have been in churches where the music is a haphazard effort. The preaching is delivered without studying "to shew thyself approved" (2 Timothy 2:15). The program is disorganized and disrespectful to the One who died for us. He deserves our best music. He deserves our best preaching. He deserves our best service.

He deserves people who wake up early to prepare to live for Him. It is the best way to get ready to face the lions.

Thirdly, we must have a praising heart. David wanted to be sure his praise was public, so he sang "among the nations." He wanted his world to know that his God is exalted above the heavens and the earth.

Sadly, we who know the Lord have been shamed to silence by our evil society. Of course, they must be allowed to proclaim their perverseness and profanity, but there is no toleration for the name of Christ.

If we are going to wind up in the lions' den, we may as well go passionately. There is no longer a reason to be cowered into silence. This pagan world is not afraid to identify with their father, so we should determine to lift up our voices and be labeled as belonging to Christ.

As Hitler was rising to power, most of the ministers and theologians in Germany supported him by their silence. Pastor Martin Niemoeller, however, refused to be quiet. For preaching the truth, he was tossed in jail.

There a co-minister visited him and implored him to soften his message. "You will be set free if you only agree to be silent on certain subjects. Why are you in jail?"

To that, Niemoeller had a simple question for his minister friend. "Then why aren't you in jail?"

Let's praise Him among the people. Let's sing to Him among our nation. May this world know that his mercy and truth are great. Let's do our best to put the pure glory of God high above this sinful earth, even if we have to do so from a lions' den.

So there is a brand new song on its way to the choir director. This time, David adds the word "Altaschith" which means "do not destroy."[53] There would be no destruction of the precious words God had given him, just as there is no destroying one of His children who is abiding under the "shadow of (his) wings."

That goes a long way to help us *encourage ourselves in the Lord.*

Chapter Eight

When the Prognosis is Dim

PSALM 30

A Psalm and Song at the dedication of the house of David.

¹ I will extol thee, O LORD; for thou hast lifted me up, and hast not made my foes to rejoice over me. ² O LORD my God, I cried unto thee, and thou hast healed me. ³ O LORD, thou hast brought up my soul from the grave: thou hast kept me alive, that I should not go down to the pit. ⁴ Sing unto the LORD, O ye saints of his, and give thanks at the remembrance of his holiness. ⁵ For his anger endureth but a moment; in his favour is life: weeping may endure for a night, but joy cometh in the morning.

⁶ And in my prosperity I said, I shall never be moved. ⁷ LORD, by thy favour thou hast made my mountain to stand strong: thou didst hide thy face, and I was troubled. ⁸ I cried to thee, O LORD; and unto the LORD I made supplication. ⁹ What profit is there in my blood, when I go down to the pit? Shall the dust praise thee? shall it declare thy truth? ¹⁰ Hear, O LORD, and have mercy upon me: LORD, be thou my helper. ¹¹ Thou hast turned for me my mourning into dancing: thou hast put off my sackcloth, and girded me with gladness; [12] *To the end that my glory may sing praise to thee, and not be silent. O LORD my God, I will give thanks unto thee for ever.*

The family had been called to the bedside. The finest doctors in the land had run out of options. The nurses could only do their best to make the patient comfortable. The sense of panic was palpable. It was time for the ultimate waiting game.

The king of Israel was lying on the bed, and only a heartbeat separated him from life and death. The very fact that he was still breathing was credited to the God that "kept (him) alive." He was tottering at the edge of the great "pit" of eternity where his only hope was a miracle. God, and only God, would have to bring him up "from the grave."

There is no indication when this crisis occurred. Perhaps David had been wounded in battle during the early days of the kingdom. Maybe the 'wars' of his later years, fought inside the palace, had caught up to him. A man like David made a lot of friends, but there were also a lot of enemies who were more than anxious to "rejoice" when he was finally gone.

"O LORD my God, I cried unto thee." What else could David do? He had spent a life cultivating a walk and a relationship with God, and as a result, he knew the LORD intimately and personally. He didn't need a massive email effort on his behalf. "The effectual fervent prayer of a righteous man availeth much" (James 5:16). He placed himself in the hands of his personal Savior.

And God "healed" him! David left no doubt: ***thou hast*** healed me...***thou hast*** brought up my soul...***thou hast*** kept me alive." There would be no sharing of the glory now. He said, "I will extol thee, O LORD," a word meaning to lift up and exalt. David wanted to lift high the name of Jehovah because He had lifted David out of the pit. The King of Kings was rightly magnified high above the King of Israel.

It was time to gather the musicians and "sing unto the LORD." We have been taught to think about eternity when we hear the words "weeping may endure for a night, but joy cometh in the morning," but for King David, that joy came on this earth. Everyone wondered if he would live to see the sunrise, but he was more than alive the next morning. God's favor on David was "life." God healed the king.

So David, help us out. How do we face foes who "rejoice over me?" What do we do when are we standing on the precipice of the "pit?" How can we go on when we are so "troubled?"

How do we *encourage ourselves in the Lord* when the prognosis is poor?

It is the reason Psalm 30 is in the Bible. The 'sweet psalmist' of Israel learned these lessons:

Let the illness remind us of our human weaknesses.

Everyone likes "prosperity." The Bible word refers to a state of abundance which includes good health.[54] We like money in the bank. We like to wake up strong and refreshed in the morning. Prosperity is the good life.

David's prosperity took many forms. As the strongest man in the world, enemies cowered before him. His military biography sounded like this: "And David went on, and grew great, and the LORD God of hosts *was* with him" (2 Samuel 5:10). When he went to battle, he was accompanied by the God of the armies and was unbeatable.

He was also incredibly wealthy. Hiram, king of Tyre, was a personal friend of David. He "sent messengers to David, and cedar trees, and carpenters, and masons: and they built David an house" (2 Samuel 5:11). David lacked for nothing.

He was respected. He "perceived that the LORD had established him king over Israel, and that he had exalted his kingdom for his people Israel's sake" (2 Samuel 5:12). God had promoted him to a higher position than any other human in the world. Most of the nations of the world feared him, and the ones who chose to oppose him did not live to regret their error.

Power. Money. Respect. Indeed he was a prosperous man, but he learned that prosperity was not all it was cracked up to be. In fact, his illness taught him that success could be very dangerous, for when he was at the top of the world, David nearly destroyed himself.

"And in my prosperity I said, I shall never be moved."

He was so affluent, so abounding, and so almighty, that he convinced himself he was invincible. There was no army that could move him. There was no king that could move him. There was no problem that could move him.

But what a massive force could not accomplish, a little germ could. The greatest battalion with their terrorizing artillery was no match for mighty David, yet an unseen virus plaguing his body had put him on his back and brought him to the precipice of eternity.

What a lesson for us! Prosperity quickly gives a false sense of security and a bloated self-confidence. While we are enjoying the good life, we quickly forget how frail our humanity truly is. We forget that it is the "favor" of God that makes the "mountain to stand strong." We are an accident away from spending the rest of our life fighting to see the next sunrise.

No one likes to be bedridden. No one enjoys the slow, painful therapy. No one wants the long, sleepless nights when a body hurts more than one thought was humanly possible. Yet, it is at these moments, where the child of God needs to ponder how weak our flesh truly is. We need Him every hour.

Let the illness help us consider the profit of our lives.

When we look at David, we are amazed at his contributions to the Word of God. His story has been retold so many times even the unsaved know of his exploits. He is easily the most prolific songwriter in world history. His kingdom was so special, we not only honor his memory, we wait for the day when he will "feed them and ... be their shepherd" once again (Ezekiel 34:23). By all accounts, David had a profitable life.

Yet David had a very different viewpoint. When he was faced with his own mortality, he asked, "What profit *is there* in my blood, when I go down to the pit?" David wondered aloud if his life counted for eternity. There was a great palace, a lot of trophies in the den, a lot of money in the bank, but he knew that would count for nothing when he met God.

"What profit is there in my life?" When lying on our backs, it is a good time to reassess the priorities of our life. Have we invested our money in the bank of Heaven? Have we invested our time in the work of the Savior? Have we invested our abilities in eternal endeavors?

Near the end of the nineteenth century, Charles Thomas Studd was an all-Englisb cricketeer for Cambridge University. We would call him an All American athlete. He used his notoriety to encourage others to surrender to serve the Lord on distant mission fields, until one day, God called him to go. Convinced that a "well done" from his Savior trumped the adoration of sports fans, C. T. Studd set out for China. "I knew that cricket would not last, and honour would not last, and nothing in this world would last, but it was worthwhile living for the world to come."

Twenty-five years later, doctors told him he was too ill to go on, yet he left for Africa where he would die serving Christ.[55] Studd left quite a legacy. He gave his impressive inheritance away for the Lord's work, wrote a number of books still read today, and influenced scores of people for the work of Christ, one of whom was Hudson Taylor.

But C. T. Studd is best known for a poem he wrote. Usually, we quote but two lines, yet the entire poem is powerful:

"Two little lines I heard one day,
Traveling along life's busy way;
Bringing conviction to my heart,
And from my mind would not depart;
Only one life, 'twill soon be past,
Only what's done for Christ will last.

Only one life, yes only one,
Soon will its fleeting hours be done;
Then, in 'that day' my Lord to meet,
And stand before His Judgement seat;
Only one life,'twill soon be past,
Only what's done for Christ will last.

Only one life, the still small voice,
Gently pleads for a better choice
Bidding me selfish aims to leave,
And to God's holy will to cleave;
Only one life, 'twill soon be past,
Only what's done for Christ will last.

Only one life, a few brief years,
Each with its burdens, hopes, and fears;
Each with its clays I must fulfill,
Living for self or in His will;

Only one life, 'twill soon be past,
Only what's done for Christ will last.

When this bright world would tempt me sore,
When Satan would a victory score;
When self would seek to have its way,
Then help me Lord with joy to say;
Only one life, 'twill soon be past,
Only what's done for Christ will last.

Give me Father, a purpose deep,
In joy or sorrow Thy word to keep;
Faithful and true what e'er the strife,
Pleasing Thee in my daily life;
Only one life, 'twill soon be past,
Only what's done for Christ will last.

Oh let my love with fervor burn,
And from the world now let me turn;
Living for Thee, and Thee alone,
Bringing Thee pleasure on Thy throne;
Only one life, 'twill soon be past,
Only what's done for Christ will last.

Only one life, yes only one,
Now let me say, "Thy will be done";
And when at last I'll hear the call,
I know I'll say "'twas worth it all";
Only one life,'twill soon be past,
Only what's done for Christ will last. "
And when I am dying, how happy I'll be,
If the lamp of my life has been burned out for Thee."[56]

Let the illness remind us to direct all the glory to God.

How good is the Lord! David knew God had raised him up, and he said, "Thou hast turned for me my mourning into dancing: thou hast put off my sackcloth, and girded me with gladness." When it looked like they were going to hold his funeral, God raised him up. His memorial service became a dedication day for the house of David.

Now that he was on the other side of the illness, David did not forget what the Lord had done. He directed all the praise to his God, gave Heaven all the credit, and sang this mighty song:

"To the end that my glory may sing praise to thee, and not be silent. O LORD my God, I will give thanks unto thee for ever."

In our times of affliction and pain, we remember how frail we truly are. We take inventory of our life in the light of eternity. We determine to use our energy in praise to Him.

It is how we *encourage ourselves in the Lord.*

Chapter Nine

The Long Tongue of the Gossip

PSALM 4

To the chief Musician on Neginoth, A Psalm of David.

¹ Hear me when I call, O God of my righteousness: thou hast enlarged me when I was in distress; have mercy upon me, and hear my prayer. ² O ye sons of men, how long will ye turn my glory into shame? how long will ye love vanity, and seek after leasing? Selah. ³ But know that the LORD hath set apart him that is godly for himself: the LORD will hear when I call unto him. ⁴ Stand in awe, and sin not: commune with your own heart upon your bed, and be still. Selah. ⁵ Offer the sacrifices of righteousness, and put your trust in the LORD.

⁶ There be many that say, Who will shew us any good? LORD, lift thou up the light of thy countenance upon us. ⁷ Thou hast put gladness in my heart, more than in the time that their corn and their wine increased. ⁸ I will both lay me down in peace, and sleep: for thou, LORD, only makest me dwell in safety.

In the fifth century BC, there lived in the country of Greece a respected statesman named Aristides. Universally praised for his character, he earned the reputation as the "best and most honorable man in Athens." His well-deserved nickname was 'Aristides the Just'.[57]

In the course of time, public opinion turned against him, and he received a vote of condemnation. When one of the Athenians was asked why he voted to condemn Aristides, he said, "I voted against him simply because I was tired of hearing him called 'the Just'."[58]

David knew the feeling.

In Psalm 4, he faced a different threat than he did in other Psalms. When battling a Saul or an Absalom, David at least knew who the enemy was. It was a little more complicated in this cantata, because the foe after David is harder to identify. Most fought with a sword. This enemy fought with a tongue.

Sometimes, Bible students try to force a setting on a Psalm where one is not given. In Psalm 4, it simply tells us that David wrote the music for the "chief musician", the choir director at the sanctuary. Perhaps the fact that no particular foe is noted indicates that the issue that prompted the song was a culmination of many years of gossip and griping. Such attacks have a way of wearing a man down.

The "neginoth" was a stringed instrument like a lyre or a harp.[59] It might seem more appropriate for David to pull out a trumpet and blast his enemies, but he took the softer approach. The dulcet notes he strummed with his fingers matched the tenderness in his heart toward those who injured him.

David's enemies, described as the "sons of men," were no ordinary folk. The phrase describes a class of wealthy, powerful, prominent landowners.[60] These citizens made it their 'ministry' to turn his "glory into shame." They would not respect the king nor the God who enthroned the king, choosing instead to spend their life humiliating David. Like too many affluent people today, they ran after vain, frivolous pleasures, and when they gathered in their small circles, they spent their time seeking "after leasing." The statement is an old English way of saying they were lying about David. The gossips told one whopper after another.

It would have been normal for David to respond: "Look at all I have done for you and this kingdom. I have been responsible for the blessing of God falling on us. I have been responsible for defeating dangerous enemies on every side. You are rich in part because I have put my life on the line." If David had allowed the critical busybodies to turn him into a bitter, angry man, we would understand. If he had turned on them and attacked them, we would conclude that he was only human.

But David had a better way. Instead of creating a blog to fuel the fight, he turned to his God: "Hear me when I call, O God of my righteousness: thou hast enlarged me *when I was* in distress; have mercy upon me, and hear my prayer."

Before he dealt with the enemy, David spoke with God. "Surely we should all speak the more boldly to men if we had more constant converse with God. He who dares to face his Maker will not tremble before the sons of men."[61]

David has learned that he cannot enter a human conflict without God's help. He needs the wisdom "from above" because it is "pure, then peaceable, gentle, *and* easy to be intreated, full of mercy and good fruits, without partiality, and without hypocrisy. And the fruit of righteousness is sown in peace of them that make peace" (James 3:17-18). Such wisdom is the perfect antidote.

He approached God with confidence because he knew he had been unjustly reproached. It is not very often that we can stand before God and claim as David did that we are personally right. In this case, David could address the God who could not be fooled and claim he had done right, knowing that his merciful Savior would hear him pray.

Slander is a powerful force. David, who was no stranger to hiding in caves as the adversary was closing in, said that the gossipers had mentally done what armies had physically done. They had put him in "distress." The frequent and powerful assaults encircled him giving him a sense there was nowhere to go and no way out, so he asked God to "enlarge" him. "Lord, I need you to show the way. I don't know where to go, and I don't know what to do. I need you to make a space for me."

And the Lord answered that prayer! David confidently said, "The LORD will hear when I call unto him." The Lord did not let him down. He gave David the perfect answer.

So David, help us out. When we are in "distress," how do we respond? When every fiber of our nature wants to retaliate and get even with those who try to turn our "glory into shame," what do we do? How do we keep from slinging mud when we are covered with it by those who "seek after leasing?"

How do we *encourage ourselves in the Lord* when the gossips are winning?

It is the reason Psalm 4 is in the Bible. David says, "When the enemy is attacking, witness to him."

What a solution! David knew the reason for their empty life and their blathering tongues, and he addressed it. They had a false view of God, and they needed to be saved.

David's foes asked this question: "Who will shew us *any* good?" With their multiple gods, they were seeking the one that would give them what they wanted, and they wanted 'good.' They cared nothing about serving God, worshipping God, or honoring God, but rather, they were interested in a god that would satisfy their selfish desires. They had an ancient version of the 'Prosperity Gospel.'

And they were lost.

So he told them to "Stand in awe, and sin not." They brazenly assailed David because there was "no fear of God before their eyes" (Romans 3:18). Had they known God, they would have been struck with the awesome fear of God, and they would have realized the offensiveness of their sin. The man who does not fear God has no reason to keep from sin.

Then he told them to "commune with your own heart upon your bed, and be still." While we think of the heart as the center of our emotional life, to David the heart was the center of reflective thinking and consideration of one's desires. It was the place where a man made his plans whether they were good or evil, wise or foolish.[62] "A good man out of the good treasure of his heart bringeth forth that which is good; and an evil man out of the evil treasure of his heart bringeth forth that which is evil: for of the abundance of the heart his mouth speaketh" (Luke 6:45).

When an evil man chooses a sinful path, he rushes on blindly without thinking. The last thing he desires is to lay on a bed at night and allow the conviction of God to upset him. He enjoys the fruit of his wickedness and does not want God to interfere with his degenerate ways. There is no interest is being still and listening to the Word of God, and the end result is a sinner who does not see the gravity of his sin.

David wanted his enemies to see their sin as God did, and if they did, they would need to "offer the sacrifices of righteousness." Presumably, those who spoke against David on Saturday night were the same ones who brought offerings to the tabernacle that very morning. They were religious, but they were not righteous. They would bring an offering that would appease their conscience, but it would not impress God. Had they listened to the conviction of God on their beds, they might have known the difference.

God wanted a righteous sacrifice. It was not enough to bring the animal or the bread or the money; it had to be accompanied by a heart of repentance. Formal trips to the altar were not the answer. He wanted obedience to His word joined to a tender heart, broken over sin. "The sacrifices of God *are* a broken spirit: a broken and a contrite heart, O God, thou wilt not despise" (Psalm 51:17).

Religion is a dangerous pacifier. Its emphasis on good works will convince a man that he is okay when he is not. A little bit of time, a little bit of money, a little bit of prayer, and the sinner can go on his merry way and live as he chooses. Next week, it will be same time, same place, and same ritual.

God said the only way to Heaven is through the righteous sacrifice of His Son:

"But now once in the end of the world hath he appeared to put away sin by the sacrifice of himself. And as it is appointed unto men once to die, but after this the judgment: So Christ was once offered to bear the sins of many; and unto them that look for him shall he appear the second time without sin unto salvation." (Hebrews 9:26-28)

What a powerful presentation of the Gospel! Sin is the problem. You are guilty. Religion and its works will not save. There is only one right way to God.

What next David?

"Put your trust in the LORD." They needed to "rely on, depend on, with the sense of being completely confident"[63] in the saving power of God. That simple message has stood the test of time. Abraham "believed in the LORD; and he counted it to him for righteousness" (Genesis 15:6). The apostle Paul told the Philippian jailor: "Believe on the Lord Jesus Christ, and thou shalt be saved" (Acts 16:31). Your religion cannot save. Your works cannot save. You need to put your trust in the only one who can save. "Put your trust in the LORD."

It is the amazing thing about soul-winners. They witness because they love the Lord who saved their soul. They witness because they love the sinner who needs Christ. But the inadvertent byproduct of soul-winning is the benefit to the child of God. When you tell a man about Christ, any bitterness you harbored toward the individual is replaced by an overwhelming concern to see him saved. Compassion replaces wrath. And when he finally trusts the Lord, an enemy becomes a brother.

It was the motivation for a Bible School teacher of a hundred years ago who wrote these words:

Give me a passion for souls, dear Lord,
A passion to save the lost;
O that Thy love were by all adored,
And welcomed at any cost.

Jesus, I long, I long to be winning
Men who are lost, and constantly sinning;
O may this hour be one of beginning
The story of pardon to tell.[64]

In our travels, I once met a missionary serving in a difficult mission field. The living conditions were brutal, the need was extraordinary, and the village was given over to sin. Humanly speaking, it was an impossible situation.

The work was slow and difficult with great opposition. One day, a wicked man in the community assaulted the missionary's young daughter. The 'police' arrested the man, but he was back on the streets within the hour. There was no justice.

The missionary, who was also a pilot, labored on for the Lord. One night he was awakened by a pounding on the door. Standing before him was the same man who had assaulted his daughter. In his arms was his young son who was running a high fever. Without medical attention, the boy would not live through the night.

The father asked the missionary if he would fly the boy to the hospital and save his life. The very man that scarred the missionary's daughter for life was now begging for the life of his own son. The missionary raced to the plane, and soon the boy was on his way to the hospital. He would live. The missionary saved the son of his greatest enemy.

Notice the change in David in Psalm 4. He started the song by groaning in "distress." He concludes the Psalm basking in the "light of (God's) countenance." His worldly enemies were happy when "their corn and their wine increased," but David had something different. The 'Prosperity Gospel' produces religious people whose happiness depends on financial circumstances, but an encouraged saint can say with David: "Thou hast put gladness in my heart." Circumstances did not make him glad. God made him glad.

How can we *encourage ourselves in the Lord?* Join your church on soul-winning night. Get some names on a list and start praying for them to be saved. Ask God to give you the boldness to testify for Him on the job or in the classroom. Leading a sinner to the Savior brings a joy and strength and encouragement that overcomes the greatest turmoil.

So there is nothing left for David to do but to "lay me down in peace, and sleep: for thou, LORD, only makest me dwell in safety." Gladness and peace instead of distress.

No wonder he went off to sleep *encouraged in the Lord*.

Chapter Ten

When Our Sin Finds Us Out

PSALM 51

To the chief Musician, A Psalm of David, when Nathan the prophet came unto him, after he had gone in to Bathsheba.

¹ Have mercy upon me, O God, according to thy lovingkindness: according unto the multitude of thy tender mercies blot out my transgressions. ² Wash me throughly from mine iniquity, and cleanse me from my sin. ³ For I acknowledge my transgressions: and my sin is ever before me. ⁴ Against thee, thee only, have I sinned, and done this evil in thy sight: that thou mightest be justified when thou speakest, and be clear when thou judgest. ⁵ Behold, I was shapen in iniquity; and in sin did my mother conceive me. ⁶ Behold, thou desirest truth in the inward parts: and in the hidden part thou shalt make me to know wisdom.

⁷ Purge me with hyssop, and I shall be clean: wash me, and I shall be whiter than snow. ⁸ Make me to hear joy and gladness; that the bones which thou hast broken may rejoice. ⁹ Hide thy face from my sins, and blot out all mine iniquities. ¹⁰ Create in me a clean heart, O God; and renew a right spirit within me. ¹¹ Cast me not away from thy presence; and take not thy holy spirit from me. ¹² Restore unto me the joy of thy salvation; and uphold me with thy free spirit. ¹³ Then will I teach transgressors thy ways; and sinners shall be converted unto thee.

¹⁴ Deliver me from bloodguiltiness, O God, thou God of my salvation: and my tongue shall sing aloud of thy righteousness. ¹⁵ O Lord, open thou my lips; and my mouth shall shew forth thy praise. ¹⁶ For thou desirest not sacrifice; else would I give it: thou delightest not in burnt offering. ¹⁷ The sacrifices of God are a broken spirit: a broken and a contrite heart, O God, thou wilt not despise. ¹⁸ Do good in thy good pleasure unto Zion: build thou the walls of Jerusalem. ¹⁹ Then shalt thou be pleased with the sacrifices of righteousness, with burnt offering and whole burnt offering: then shall they offer bullocks upon thine altar.

"Thou art the man."

David never saw it coming.

For a solid year he had fooled a kingdom and no one knew. No one had figured it out. To the average citizen, David came out looking like the good guy. He had comforted the bereaved widow, had gone so far as to take this wife of the military hero as his own, and now God had 'blessed' them with a little baby. He had sinned and gotten away with it.

And then came the words: *"Thou art the man."*

Nathan the prophet came to King David with a story. A wealthy man in his kingdom had taken advantage of a poor man. Though he possessed "exceeding many flocks and herds," he "took the poor man's lamb, and dressed it for the (traveller) that was come to him" (2 Samuel 12:2,4). It was all the poor man had. He treated the lamb like a "daughter."

David was furious. "The man that hath done this *thing* shall surely die: And he shall restore the lamb fourfold, because he did this thing, and because he had no pity" (2 Samuel 12:5-6).

Then Nathan blindsided him:

"Thou art the man."

I wonder how many Psalms David wrote during that year? I suspect the number was zero. When a man's conscience is thrashing him, the last thing he wants to do is sing. David's sin had closed his mouth, and the only way he would ever "shew forth thy praise" would be if the Lord would "open (his) lips" (Psalm 51:15).

Once again, the Bible proved itself true. Even King David discovered his sin would ultimately "find (him) out" (Numbers 32:23). "The way of transgressors *is* hard" (Proverbs 13:15). "There is no respect of persons with God" (Romans 2:11). David was not the exception.

David found himself at a critical juncture in his life. When sin is exposed, humans usually respond with a denial. "I didn't do it; I wouldn't do it; I couldn't do it." There is often a pretense of rage directed at the 'Nathan' who exposed the wickedness. "How dare you insinuate such a thing!" When the culmination of evidence is too great, the guilty man tries to minimize the sin. "It only happened once; it is not a big a deal as you are making it out to be." Next, there is a reluctant admitting of the wrong and the appropriate 'crocodile tears.' Then one morning, the man wakes up convinced this is the day "I can put it all behind me."

Sin doesn't work like that.

When Nathan the prophet pointed the finger of conviction at David, the true character of the king came out. He did not respond with rage, rebuttal, or revenge; he responded with Psalm 51. When someone wonders how a man who committed the horrible sins of David could be called a 'man after God's own heart', the answer is Psalm 51. It is one thing to rejoice and sing when one is right with God and blessed by God. It is something entirely different to respond to sin like David did.

I suspect Nathan's convicting message meant relief for David. There are many men that don't mind playing the game of the hypocrite, and some are quite good at it, but David was different. His life was a sham. His sin was "ever before" him. Everywhere he went he was haunted by the sin. Every time he led the nation in worship to God, he must have kicked himself internally for his phoniness. Now the secret was out. He didn't have to play the game any longer.

"Thou art the man."

David responded, "I have sinned against the LORD" (2 Samuel 12:13).

One can imagine the scene in the royal throne room. The news reporters are scurrying to be the first to tweet the announcement. There are cries of anger and tears of sorrow as emotions are erupting. It probably did not take very long before the nearly five million residents from Dan to Beersheba knew it. He was exposed and embarrassed.

"Thou art the man."
"I have sinned against the LORD."

The political advisors must have been apoplectic figuring out how to control the damage and limit the news flow. The pundits on both sides could not get to the microphones fast enough. His foes were laughing, his friends were weeping, and in distant palaces, enemies were plotting his downfall.

David did the only thing he knew to do. He grabbed a parchment, and for the first time perhaps in a long time, God gave him a song. God is about to turn the lowest moment in David's life into an eternal highlight. Only He can do that.

The king began to write. I suspect the tears were rolling down his cheeks as God gave him the words to Psalm 51, yet, those were not tears of embarrassment, shame, or selfishness. Those tears flowed because of what David had done to God. He was not ashamed for his own selfish reasons; he was ashamed that he had disgraced his Savior.

So David, help us out. When our sins are "ever before" us, what do we do? How do we make things right when we have wronged "thee, (and) thee only?" What do we do when we finally realize that we were "shapen in iniquity," and conceived "in sin?"

How do we *encourage ourselves in the Lord* when we have lost the "joy of thy salvation?"

It is the reason Psalm 51 is in the Bible. *"The sacrifices of God are a broken spirit: a broken and a contrite heart, O God, thou wilt not despise."*

We need to see our sin from God's point of view.

We love to tell ourselves that sin is a private matter. The pundits in David's day may well have sounded like the defenders of former President Bill Clinton: "This is a private matter between two consenting adults. It is none of our business."

That simply was not true. When David committed adultery, he sinned against Bathsheba, against her husband Uriah, against his own family, and against his nation. He gave "great occasion to the enemies of the LORD to blaspheme" (2 Samuel 12:14). There were great privileges extended to the king of Israel, but there was also greater responsibility. "For unto whomsoever much is given, of him shall be much required" (Luke 12:48).

But notice what David said in verse 4:

"Against thee, thee only, have I sinned, and done this evil in thy sight."

Some are offended at this statement. They think that David is belittling Bathsheba and Uriah, but that misses the point. David is exposing the ugliness of his sin in the ultimate manner. If it were only against another man or woman, if it were only a private matter, it would be evil enough. But David knew his sin was ultimately an act of rebellion against God. All of the damage done to his human counterparts was minuscule in comparison to the disgrace he inflicted upon the name of God.

God is the One who laid out the ground rule: "Thou shalt not commit adultery" (Exodus 20:14). While our sins may offend others and cause them to stumble, ultimately, we sin against the Holy God of the Bible. It is an act of defiance against Him, and He is the only one that can remedy that rebellion.

David saw sin differently than we do. We have our human ideas of justice. We want to look the other way and pretend it never happened. We do everything we can to rename sin and minimize its effects. But David recognized that God had every right to judge both sin and sinner: "that thou mightest be justified when thou speakest, *and* be clear when thou judgest." The Holy Judge of Heaven always judges justly. He is correct and blameless when He pronounces His decision. It would not matter what the opinion polls would say about the king. God's view was the only one that counted.

In 1855, a London doctor named William Palmer was found guilty of murder in one of the most notorious cases of the 19th century. Using strychnine, Palmer poisoned his wife, his brother, his mother-in-law, his four children, and a close friend, so that he might collect money from life insurance policies. He then lost the money gambling on horses. Charles Dickens called Palmer "the greatest villain that ever stood in the Old Bailey".[65]

On June 14, 1856, Palmer was publicly hanged. The next morning, Charles Spurgeon stood in the pulpit of the New Park Street Chapel and preached these words:

Yesterday was to me a day of deep solemnity; a pressure rested on my mind throughout the whole of it, which I could not by any possibility remove, for at every hour I remembered that

*during that day one of the most fallen of my fellow-creatures was
launched into an unknown world, and made to stand before his
Maker, Some might have witnessed his execution without tears; I
think I could not even have thought of it for long together
without weeping, at the terrible idea of a man so guilty, about to
commence that endless period of unmingled misery, which is the
horrible doom of the impenitent, which God hath prepared for
sinners. Yesterday morning the sun saw a sight which sickened it
—the sight of a man launched, by a judicial process, into
eternity, for guilt which has rendered him infamous, and which
will stamp his name with disgrace as long as it shall be
remembered.*[66]

It would be hard to imagine a fate worse than a public
execution, yet William Palmer had an appointment far
more terrifying than the sentence he received from an
earthly judge. He instantly met the God of the Bible, whose
judgments are always just and always correct. His
problems did not end when he died-they only began.

We need to understand what God is not looking for.

In our society, the default response to exposed sin is
religion. Some people go to the confessional booth. Some
people walk down an aisle and cover the altar with tears.
Some people make a 'profession of faith'. Some people
give an offering. Religion is a great salve to soothe a
convicted conscience.

David was in a mess, and there were no religious
solutions. "For thou desirest not sacrifice; else would I give
it: thou delightest not in burnt offering" (Psalm 51:16). He

had committed an intentional sin of adultery, and the law demanded a serious consequence:

"But the soul that doeth ought presumptuously, whether he be born in the land, or a stranger, the same reproacheth the LORD; and that soul shall be cut off from among his people." (Numbers 15:30)

Sins such as adultery or murder were not provided for in sacrificial instructions, and the execution of the adulterer or the murderer was required.[67] There would be no minister on the other side of the booth claiming to absolve David. There would be no generous gift that could change the outcome here. There would be no special sacrifice that David could bring to make God forget. He was in deep trouble.

David "was shapen in iniquity." The events that comprise this story were hardly an accident. David did not simply 'fall off the wagon' and make a 'mistake'. From the moment he was conceived, he was a sinner destined to die. "Wherefore, as by one man sin entered into the world, and death by sin; and so death passed upon all men, for that all have sinned" (Romans 5:12).

The Cross of Jesus paints the ultimate picture of religion's feebleness. If works and prayers and gifts could provide the answer for sin, there would be no reason for the Savior to suffer such an inglorious, horrific death. "Wherefore when he cometh into the world, he saith, Sacrifice and offering thou wouldest not, but a body hast thou prepared me: In burnt offerings and *sacrifices* for sin thou hast had no pleasure" (Hebrews 10:5-6). He had to die because God is not looking for a feeble act of religion.

We need to understand what God is looking for.

As David rejects the thought that religious sacrifices could appease God, he expresses in two verses the reaction that the Lord was looking for. The first is verse six, where the Bible says that God desires "truth in the inward parts." Notice that God does not 'demand' truth; He 'desires' truth. He is delighted and pleased[68] when His creation determines to forsake the gamesmanship and hypocrisy that religion encourages. He is not looking for outward profession. He is looking for inward purity.

The second verse is Psalm 51:17: "The sacrifices of God *are* a broken spirit: a broken and a contrite heart, O God, thou wilt not despise." Before God could rebuild David, he had to break him. He had to break his pride, his arrogance, and his stubbornness, and with the words: *"Thou art the man,"* David's cocoon of hypocrisy was crushed and shattered. God found a heart that was "contrite" (torn to pieces).

We are taught to believe that a broken heart is a bad thing, but with God, it is a necessary thing. When our heart is broken, we are no longer full of ourselves. We have realized the seriousness of our sin and the broken fellowship with God. We find ourselves quiet and thoughtful before Him. We are ashamed of what we have done.

How amazing is God's solution! Religion offers its external sacraments, offerings, prayers, and robes, but God is looking for an internal, simple solution. One does not need a seminary degree to comprehend. God is looking for a genuine, broken heart, and He promised that He would never "despise" someone coming in such a condition.

We need to take responsibility for our sin.

When Nathan pointed the finger of conviction at David, it did not take him a long time to respond. He didn't wait for the second verse of the invitation song to step out.

The first person pronoun is used ten times in the first three verses of Psalm 51. David left absolutely no doubt as to who was responsible for the sin. "My transgressions...mine iniquity...my sin."

Nathan said, *"Thou art the man."*

In no uncertain terms, David agreed, "I am the man."

The word "acknowledge" in verse three describes his willingness to know and admit that what God said is true. It may seem patently obvious that he knew what he had done was sinful, but very humans consider their sin as such. Rare is the man that is willing to look at his life and acknowledge his sin in the light of God and His word.

There is something refreshing about his response. There are 343 powerful words found in Psalm 51, but there is one word that is not found in the song-the word *'but'*. He never says, "I have sinned, *but* what about Bathsheba. I have sinned, *but* you need to understand the pressures of my job. I have sinned, *but* it is not as bad as people say it is."

No 'ifs,' no 'buts,' and no exceptions. David was taking complete responsibility and ownership for his sin.

It is important to see the various words David employed to describe his sin. Transgressions are an act of rebellion against God.[69] Iniquities refer to the "state of guilt that results from sin,[70] while the basic meaning of the word 'sin' means to miss a mark or a way.[71] He wasn't done. In verse 4 he refers to his affair with Bathsheba and his subsequent acts as "evil," and in verse 14 he uses the word "bloodguiltiness." The coroner's report stated that Uriah died of a Hittite arrow, but David knew better. "I am guilty of the shedding of that man's blood."

We need to know what only God can do.

As King of Israel, David lived an incredible life. He had the wealth to buy anything he desired. He had the power to command his world to do his bidding. But as a broken man, David realized there was a work that only God could do.

In verses 7-12, David sounds like a helpless child. He is reduced to begging God to accomplish what he cannot do on his own. It is a difficult thing for a man to admit he is unable to do something for himself. It is humbling to acknowledge that we are not as mighty as we pretend to be.

Look at these requests: " Purge me...wash me...make me...create in me...cast me not away...restore unto me...uphold me." There is a level of desperation here. When David was confronted with his sin, he faced the realization that there was no human work that he could do to solve the problem. *"Thou art the man"* crushed every notion of human effort and invention.

Religion has created purgatory, but David knew only God could purge him. Ministers lower people into a basin and inform them that the water will wash away their sin, but David knew only God could wash him. Pills, prescriptions, philosophies, and psychologies cannot make a new man, but David knew that God could.

Only the God of creation can make a dirty heart clean. Only the God of all mercies can receive a sinner who deserves to be cast off. Only the God of joy can restore the joy of salvation. Only the God of grace can uphold a man and safely bring him home.

It is the result of a man or woman being confronted with their sin. Until we know how dark it is, we will never be able to comprehend what God is able to do. *"Thou art the man"* was truly a blessing in disguise.

We need to trust God to do what only He can do.

There is a lot to admire about David's humility and contrition, but if a human will ever be restored, God has to do all the work. As we cannot save ourselves, so we cannot cleanse ourselves. The phrase is found in verse fourteen: "Deliver me." Someone stronger than David would have to snatch him out of the disaster he had created. Like a man drowning in a lake or a woman pleading from a burning building, King David needed God to rescue him.[72]

There are six occasions in the song where David directly addresses the Lord, and he usually does so with the phrase, "O God." It is not difficult to imagine David pleading the name of God. He has shamed his Lord and dragged the holy name of God through the mud, so he is trying to find words to accurately express the remorse in his soul. He wants God to "open (his) lips" so that his "mouth (could) shew forth (His) praise." The tears may well have been running down his cheeks; they were surely running from his heart.

And the Lord delivered him! It is true that the consequences of his sin would be felt until the day he died, but it is also true that the fellowship with his God was real again. Years later, God was still blessing Israel on account of David: "Nevertheless for David's sake did the LORD his God give him a lamp in Jerusalem, to set up his son after him, and to establish Jerusalem: Because David did *that which was* right in the eyes of the LORD, and turned not aside from any *thing* that he commanded him **all the days** of his life, save only in the matter of Uriah the Hittite" (1 Kings 15:4-5).

God washed him. God cleansed him. God purged him. God created a clean heart. God renewed a right spirit. God restored the joy of his salvation.

And God blotted out David's sin. That is a glorious truth. When we hear the word 'blot,' we might imagine an antique ink blotter covering a secretary's mistake. Perhaps we picture the little bottle of white-out used with a typewriter. A Texas woman named Bette Nesmith turned that little bottle into a fifty million dollar business.

But the Bible word "blot" has a different meaning. Centuries ago, the cost of a writing parchment was prohibitively expensive. When a writer made an error, they would take a moist sponge and carefully wash the mistake away. When the parchment dried, it would be impossible to tell that the mistake was ever there. The error was wiped out.[73]

So it was with David's sin. By the mercy of God, it was washed away and removed so that there was no record of the sin ever existing. In God's account book, sins are not painted over, nor are they erased. They are completely removed.

In 1927, the songwriter, Merrill Dunlop, was crossing the Atlantic on an ocean liner called *The Leviathan*. As he sat on the deck and watched the rolling waves, he began to think of his God who had removed his sins and buried them in the sea. Soon, he was writing these words:

What a wondrous message in God's Word!
My sins are blotted out, I know!
If I trust in His redeeming blood,
My sins are blotted out, I know!

Once my heart was black, but now what joy;
My sins are blotted out, I know!
I have peace that nothing can destroy;
My sins are blotted out, I know!

I shall stand some day before my King;
My sins are blotted out, I know!
With the ransomed host I then shall sing:
"My sins are blotted out, I know!"

My sins are blotted out, I know!
My sins are blotted out, I know!

They are buried in the depths of the deepest sea:
My sins are blotted out, I know![74]

So David calls for the chief musician and informs him that God has given him another song. It may well have been a long time since he had penned some words. I wonder if the choir director assumed he would never write again.

"My tongue shall sing aloud of thy righteousness." His actions certainly reverberated throughout the land, but now he wants his song to be unrestrained. It is fascinating that he wants to sing of "righteousness" instead of 'mercy.' One would assume that David would accentuate and extol the love of His God, yet, he shouted of God's righteousness. When God forgives, we know that He is compassionate, merciful, and full of grace, but we usually do not consider that His forgiveness is also right. Certainly, we don't deserve it, but when God forgives, He is keeping His promise and His word. It is the reason 1 John 1:9 reminds us that His forgiveness is based on His faithfulness and His justice.

I suppose that David never thought he would see the day when he could once again be encouraged in the Lord, but God is able to break and then make. We can be restored to Him. We can know His mercy. We can be strong again, even when we have sinned against God.

It is how we *encourage ourselves in the Lord.*

Chapter Eleven

Abandoned By Family

PSALM 3

A Psalm of David, when he fled from Absalom his son.

[1] LORD, how are they increased that trouble me! many are they that rise up against me. [2] Many there be which say of my soul, There is no help for him in God. Selah. [3] But thou, O LORD, art a shield for me; my glory, and the lifter up of mine head.

[4] I cried unto the LORD with my voice, and he heard me out of his holy hill. Selah. [5] I laid me down and slept; I awaked; for the LORD sustained me. [6] I will not be afraid of ten thousands of people, that have set themselves against me round about. [7] Arise, O LORD; save me, O my God: for thou hast smitten all mine enemies upon the cheek bone; thou hast broken the teeth of the ungodly. [8] Salvation belongeth unto the LORD: thy blessing is upon thy people. Selah.

The enemy seemed invincible and innumerable. We only need a quick glance at Psalm 3 to get the picture.

"Increased...many...many...ten thousands of people...round about." The repetition of the word "many" pictures a force that is multiplying against David. The Baptist preacher of yesteryear, Charles Spurgeon, put it like this: "Troubles always come in flocks. Sorrow hath a numerous family."[75] How right he was. As dangerous as the scenario may have been at that moment in time, it was actually an escalating situation growing worse by the moment. David's life was hanging in the balance.

That must have been a hard lesson for the king. Political leaders surround themselves with counselors who tell them what they want to hear. Few are the advisors who tell it like it is, and fewer are the leaders willing to listen. When someone finally told David that "the conspiracy was strong...(and that) the people increased continually" against him (2 Samuel 15:12), such rejection must have shaken him to the core. He was now in a war he didn't want to fight, but it was a war nonetheless. There are no less than nine military terms in these eight verses.

The situation on the ground was deteriorating. The enemies were not only gaining strength, they were closing in "round about." When David said, "They trouble me," he did not use the normal word expected to describe an enemy. Instead, he used a word to depict a foe who was surrounding him and cutting off the paths of escape:

"One can almost sense the panic as the psalmist, turning this way and that, seeking a way out, sees only the multitude of enemies pressing ever closer, about to overwhelm. Perhaps the image is of being tightly bound and unable to escape—something

like what the victim of the boa constrictor experiences as the relentless coils draw ever tighter, cutting off escape and crushing life."[76]

But there was something in this confrontation that was far worse. Had David been facing the Philistines, the Moabites, the Syrians, the Ammonites, the Amalekites, or the Edomites, he was confident that his God would "preserve" him "whithersoever" he would go (2 Samuel 8:14). But this was different. The superscript (the title of the Psalm) states it like this: "A Psalm of David, when he fled from Absalom his son."[77]

David was now at war with his own son.

It was the cunning and crafty Absalom who "stole the hearts of the men of Israel" (2 Samuel 15:6), and now he had made the choice to "rise up against" David. The subterfuge had become an open rebellion led by a diabolical son rising against his father. Yet, as painful as that insurrection must have been, the cruelest truth hits David in Psalm 3:2: "Many *there be* which say of my soul, *There is* no help for him in God."

The taunts of Absalom and his forces were not simply against David, they were against God. Where David is crying to his personal Savior, (as noted by the use of the name of Jehovah LORD), Absalom uses a generic name for God. He could have used that name to speak about the God of the Bible, Baal, Chemosh, or any other pagan deity. They were all the same to him. To this rebel, he was his own god.

His son was not only a rebel, he was also lost. He could never say as David could that the LORD is "my God" (Psalm 3:7). Absalom did not have a personal Savior, and when he died, he went to Hell. It is the reason David wailed, "O my son Absalom, my son, my son Absalom! would God I had died for thee, O Absalom, my son, my son!" (2 Samuel 18:33). There are not many things more heartbreaking than knowing your own child has rejected God and His Salvation for the final time.

Perhaps you have experienced the pain of David. You may have privately cried out like David, "My son, my son...would God I had died for thee...my son, my son!" You may have known the torment of a son or daughter you love that has abandoned the Lord.

So David, help us out. What do you do when you are out of options? How do you respond when hope is gone? What can you do when you own son is breaking your heart?

How do we *encourage ourselves in the Lord* when our loved ones have risen up against us?

It is the reason Psalm 3 is in the Bible. The sweet psalmist of Israel says: "I laid me down and slept."

What a reaction! Notice his doctors did not give David a bottle of sleeping pills. Notice that he was not under medical orders to rest. He laid *himself* down and went right off to sleep.

Years of walking with God was paying off for David. His past battles with bears, lions, and giants taught him that his God was more than strong enough for this test. The countless hours of singing and filling his heart with the Word of God would now carry him through the darkest hour. His relationship to God was not religion to him. It was real.

In the darkest hour of his life, David knew what would happen next because he saw what God had done in the past. Psalm 3 is almost like reading a newspaper account after the fact. It didn't matter how dark the night, nor how foreboding the circumstances, David had no doubts about his God.

"But thou, O LORD, *art* a shield for me; my glory, and the lifter up of mine head." There were many different shields a soldier in David's day could use, but this particular kind of shield would protect a soldier entirely: above, beneath, around, without, and within. The enemy was "round about," but so was the shield.

The LORD was his "glory." For a king accustomed to human praise and adulation, it would be a difficult thing to find himself running for his life and sleeping in a humble cave. David knew that human, kingly glory was fleeting. The only honor that mattered was the glory from above. He could point to the lost city behind him and say, "That city is not my glory. That palace is not my glory. Some crown is not my glory. The Lord is my glory. His honor is all I need."

One of the most important lessons David learned was to allow the Lord to be the "lifter up of mine head." When someone was said to 'lift up their own head,' it was a way of describing extreme arrogance and haughtiness. But David knew what Daniel knew. It is God who "removeth kings, and setteth up kings" (Daniel 2:21). Asaph sang it like this: "For promotion *cometh* neither from the east, nor from the west, nor from the south. But God *is* the judge: he putteth down one, and setteth up another" (Psalm 75:6-7). God gave him the kingdom in the past, took the kingdom in the present, and was well able to give him the kingdom back in the future.

David genuinely believed that Absalom was no match for Almighty God, and an incredibly complex and perplexing situation suddenly presented David with a mighty simple solution. "I cried...he heard...I laid me down and slept." How we wish we had that kind of confidence in God!

David slept because he knew that God heard his cry from his "holy hill." The holy hill was back where David used to live in Jerusalem. Absalom thought he had control but how wrong he was. God stilled ruled. The holy hill, (known now as the Temple Mount), was the very spot where God had coronated David as the king. David knew where God was, and more importantly, he knew that God knew where he was.

So he went to sleep trusting God, and when he woke up the next morning, it was to a day where he knew that God would sustain him. If God could get him through the night, then God would get him through the next day.

There are lessons here for us. If we will *encourage ourselves in the Lord*, then we must be able to learn the lessons that God has taught us in the past. Those lessons are the building blocks of faith for the Christian.

David was a master at this. When it was time to battle Goliath, he told King Saul, "The LORD that delivered me out of the paw of the lion, and out of the paw of the bear, he will deliver me out of the hand of this Philistine" (1 Samuel 17:37). There was no doubt. God had proven Himself in the past, and He would do it again.

It is the same thing in Psalm 3. Past lessons taught him that his God had "smitten all (his) enemies *upon* the cheek bone; thou hast broken the teeth of the ungodly." He is saying, "I know that God will take care of me here, because He has taken care of me in the past. I have seen him defeat my enemies so many times that I have no doubts that he will do it again."

Smiting an enemy on the cheek bone was an expression of publicly humiliating an enemy.[78] A mouth full of broken teeth meant Absalom would no longer be able to say, "Oh that I were made judge in the land, that every man which hath any suit or cause might come unto me, and I would do him justice!" (2 Samuel 15:4). God knew how to shame the enemy. God knew how to silence the enemy.

Be it one Goliath or tens of thousands of enemies, David knew what was going to happen. The track record of God's power and care taught him that "Salvation *belongeth* unto the LORD." So he said, "Arise, O LORD; save me, O my God."

When the Israelites broke camp in the wilderness, the cloud of God led them. At that time, Moses would cry out, "Rise up, LORD, and let thine enemies be scattered; and let them that hate thee flee before thee" (Numbers 10:35). That phrase of Moses became the battle cry of Israel in the Old Testament. When going to war, they needed the LORD to go before them, defeat the enemy, and give them victory.

There are thirteen occasions where they cry for God to rise up and deliver them.[79]

From a human standpoint, it paints an impressive picture. Imagine God rising to champion His people. The lowly and feeble Absaloms of this world can only watch in horror as the mighty defender fills the sky. The decrepit instruments of war melt in their hands before the gleaming sword of God. Their complex war strategies are mocked by his eminent brilliance.

Well could David have echoed the words of another politician born 28 centuries later. Sir Robert Grant, the appointed Governor of Bombay, India, penned it like this:

O worship the King, all-glorious above,
And gratefully sing His pow'r and His love;
Our Shield and Defender, the Ancient of Days,
Pavilioned in splendor and girded with praise.

O tell of His might, O sing of His grace,
Whose robe is the light, whose canopy space;
His chariots of wrath the deep thunderclouds form,
And dark is His path on the wings of the storm.

Frail children of dust, and feeble as frail,
In thee do we trust, nor find thee to fail;
Thy mercies how tender, how firm to the end!
Our Maker, Defender, Redeemer and Friend.[80]

So he laid down and slept! Of course he did! And when we finally let the lessons of faith get hold of our hearts and our lives, we will sleep peacefully as well.

A mother and her four-year-old daughter were preparing to retire for the night. The child was afraid of the dark, and the mother, on this occasion alone with the child, felt fearful also. When the light was out, the child caught a glimpse of the moon outside the window. "Mother," she asked, "is the moon God's light?"

"Yes," said the mother.

The next question was, "Will God put out His light and go to sleep?"

The mother replied, "No, my child, God never goes to sleep."

Then out of the simplicity of a child's faith, she said, "Well, as long as God is awake, there is no sense both of us staying awake."[81]

I love the way the commentator John Phillips put it:

So David, encouraging himself in the Lord, seizes his pen and begins to jot down the thoughts that come crowding into his mind. Joab yawns, sits up, and casts a fierce eye around the camp to make sure the guard is awake and alert. He glances over at the king. There he sits, propped up on his bedroll, writing away as though he were safe in his study at home. "What's he doing now?" wonders Joab.

Joab's jaw drops. The fugitive king has been writing a hymn — and with Absalom's forces mustering by the thousand only a hill or two away! Just then David glances up and catches Joab's eye.

David's smile broadens. "Here, Joab, listen to this: 'Lord, how are they increased that trouble me!'" He reads to Joab the stanzas of what has been handed down to us as the third psalm. Such is the scene.[82]

Trusting the track record of God is how we *encourage ourselves in the Lord.*

Chapter Twelve

Wilderness

PSALM 63

A Psalm of David, when he was in the wilderness of Judah.

¹ O God, thou art my God; early will I seek thee: my soul thirsteth for thee, my flesh longeth for thee in a dry and thirsty land, where no water is; ² To see thy power and thy glory, so as I have seen thee in the sanctuary.

³ Because thy lovingkindness is better than life, my lips shall praise thee. ⁴ Thus will I bless thee while I live: I will lift up my hands in thy name. ⁵ My soul shall be satisfied as with marrow and fatness; and my mouth shall praise thee with joyful lips: ⁶ When I remember thee upon my bed, and meditate on thee in the night watches.

⁷ Because thou hast been my help, therefore in the shadow of thy wings will I rejoice. ⁸ My soul followeth hard after thee: thy right hand upholdeth me. ⁹ But those that seek my soul, to destroy it, shall go into the lower parts of the earth. ¹⁰ They shall fall by the sword: they shall be a portion for foxes. ¹¹ But the king shall rejoice in God; every one that sweareth by him shall glory: but the mouth of them that speak lies shall be stopped.

As a young man, David's flights from Saul led him to many a cave. As an old man, David's running from Absalom led him to the wilderness. A cave is not exactly the 'Hilton,' but it sure beats the wilderness.

We know that Psalm 63 rehearses events near the end of David's life. Verse eleven informs us that he is now a king, yet, the fact that he is in the wilderness of Judah pinpoints these days to his fleeing from his rebel son, Absalom.

It is hard to watch an old man in the wilderness. It is the time of life that should be a harvest of blessing for a life of honoring Christ, yet all too often, it turns into a cacophony of heartbreak, loneliness, and bitterness. Like David, an old man may have fond memories of the past days of God's power and glory "in the sanctuary," but that 'sanctuary' has been replaced by a "dry and thirsty" wilderness. The refreshing streams of the glorious house of worship have given way to the land "where no water is."

It is almost painful to hear a broken man cry out from the desert: "My soul thirsteth for thee, my flesh longeth for thee." When David was in the cave, he instinctively knew that a conclusion to the conflict was imminent. He might live, or he might die. Either way, an answer was soon to come. But the wilderness doesn't seem to have a border. It stretches on as far as the eye can see. A man in the wilderness often wonders if he will ever find relief from his pain, sorrow, and loneliness.

So David, help us out. What do we do when we find ourselves in the "wilderness" of life? How do we survive the desolate wastelands where we "thirst for thee?" Is there any hope for a man parched on the inside and outside, whose "soul" and "flesh" are yearning for the fellowship of days that seem to be gone forever? What do we do when all we want is a refreshing drink from the springs of living water only to discover there is "no water?"

How do we *encourage ourselves in the Lord* in the "wilderness" of life?

It is the reason Psalm 63 is in the Bible. *"O God, thou art my God; early will I seek thee."*

Notice that even in the wilderness, David did not stop singing and praying. It is true his songs and prayers sounded much differently than they did in the joyous house of God, but he praises and pleads nonetheless. When we are trudging through the desert sands of life, often times the last thing we want to do is pray and worship, yet these are the hours where such a walk with God is even more crucial. We cannot stop living for Christ because life has thrown us a curve.

David recognized that even in the wilderness, He is the God of "power" and "glory." Even in the wilderness, His "lovingkindness *is* better than life." Even in the wilderness, He satisfies with "marrow and fatness."[83]

Had David thrown in the towel and quit on God, we would understand. His selfish, cold-blooded boy had stolen "the hearts of the men of Israel" (2 Samuel 15:6) with calculated criticisms of his dad. His one time counselor and friend, Ahithophel, had turned traitor. He even endured the denunciations and curses of a lowlife named Shimei. It seemed as if the whole world were against him.

He responded by building what we often call a devotional life. "Early will I seek thee." Instead of lying on his bed in self-pity, David wakes up before the alarm goes off and meets his Lord. When I was a teenager, my youth pastor called it a 'quiet time.' A personal time in the Bible and in prayer will accomplish something that sermons cannot. It will soothe the heart in a way that Gospel music won't. It will bring a real and lasting peace that friends and confidants cannot provide.

"Early will I seek thee." There is a diligence to this statement. David was not going to read a chapter or two and then go on his merry way. He carved out time in his daily life where he would go and find God. He did not ask God to meet him at his own level. He sought out God at His level.

This was an intense time of the day for David. Living in the wilderness gives a different perspective on the importance of a drop of water. "The one who has crossed the desert on foot knows the life-and-death importance of water sources and keeps an intent lookout for any evidences of moisture. In the same way, the psalmist is keeping an intent lookout for any evidence of God's saving presence."[84]

When he would lie down at night, he was still thinking and remembering God. When he took his turn guarding the city during one of the night watches, he passed those four hours "meditating on thee." Meditation is a fascinating concept in the Bible. Many religions teach their followers to have a time where they empty their mind in meditation, but the Bible teaches just the opposite. Mediation is not a time to empty our minds, but rather, a time to fill our minds with the Word of God.

The 'quiet time' worked! Those early moments spent with God and the rising sun built a relationship where David could say, "O God, thou art my God." The late night hours created a confidence that God would "uphold" David and destroy his foes. Even in the lonely wilderness, David is on the victory side!

A Baptist pastor in the mid 1800's, Vernon Charlesworth, had a great love for children. He joined Charles Spurgeon in establishing an orphanage for poor, abused boys and girls. He gave forty-six years of his life to these children.

Along the way, Pastor Charlesworth wrote numerous hymns. On one occasion, while reading Psalm 32:7, he was prompted to pen a song that would stand the test of time. "Thou *art* my hiding place; thou shalt preserve me from trouble; thou shalt compass me about with songs of deliverance." The words he wrote quickly became a favorite song of fishermen off the northern coast of England. They were often heard singing them as they approached the harbor in times of storm.

Decades later, the saints of God still love to sing:

The Lord's our rock, in Him we hide,
A shelter in the time of storm;

Secure whatever ill betide,
A shelter in the time of storm.

A shade by day, defense by night,
A shelter in the time of storm;
No fears alarm, no foes affright,
A shelter in the time of storm.

The raging storms may round us beat,
A shelter in the time of storm;
We'll never leave our safe retreat,
A shelter in the time of storm.

O rock divine, O refuge dear,
A shelter in the time of storm;
Be Thou our helper ever near,
A shelter in the time of storm.

Oh, Jesus is a rock in a weary land,
A weary land, a weary land;
Oh, Jesus is a rock in a weary land,
A shelter in the time of storm.[85]

The superscript does not tell us where David sent this song. While most of the others were off to the choir director, perhaps David kept this one close at hand. It was, after all, the song of his personal devotions. It was the song that came from those quiet times between David and his God. It was the song that sustained him in the wilderness.

Such a song is how we can *encourage ourselves in the Lord.*

Chapter Thirteen
For Ever and Ever!

1 SAMUEL 30:6

...but David encouraged himself in the LORD his God.

The future could not have been brighter for the twenty-six year old preacher, Luther Bridgers. He had a wife, three little ones, and multiple opportunities to preach for his Savior.

After a series of meetings, they journeyed to a reunion with Mrs. Bridgers' family in Harrodsburg, Kentucky. It was late at night when they finally retired. In the early morning hours, a neighbor awoke and saw the homestead blazing with fire. Luther and his in-laws escaped the inferno. Sadly, after realizing his wife and sons were trapped in the flames, it was too late to rescue them. Bridgers had to be restrained as the walls of the house began to crumble. What started as a joyous reunion would end with four funerals.

The young preacher was crushed. With deep waters of sorrow encompassing him, he remembered his God promised to give a "song in the night" (Psalm 77:6). Months before the tragedy would change his life, God had given him a song. The message was now more relevant than ever:

There's within my heart a melody,
Jesus whispers sweet and low,
"Fear not, I am with thee - peace, be still,"
In all of life's ebb and flow.

All my life was wrecked by sin and strife.
Discord filled my heart with pain.
Jesus swept across the broken strings,
Stirred the slumbering chords again.

Feasting on the riches of His grace,
Resting 'neath His sheltering wing,
Always looking on His smiling face
That is why I shout and sing.

Though sometimes He leads through waters deep;
Trials fall across the way;
Though sometimes the path seem rough and steep;
See His footprints all the way.

Soon He's coming back to welcome me
Far beyond the starry sky;

I shall wing my flight to worlds unknown;
I shall reign with Him on high.

Jesus, Jesus, Jesus! Sweetest name I know!
Fills my every longing, keeps me singing as I go.[86]

The songs given to David tell quite the story. From the days when the shepherd boy would wander the Judean hillsides glorying in the handiwork of God to the last moments of his storied life, the 'sweet psalmist of Israel' experienced some of the greatest heights and some of the deepest canyons that a human has ever known. Through it all, he learned to walk with his King.

The final Psalm of David in our Bible is Psalm 145. Whether it is the final song he wrote in his lifetime or not, it is the final time we get to hear from him. The last words of the last song say:

"My mouth shall speak the praise of the LORD: and let all flesh bless his holy name for ever and ever." (Psalm 145:21)

What a fitting end for an exemplary life! Through all the battles and struggles without and within, David wanted his lasting testimony to be one of praise to Jehovah. To his dying breath, he looked forward to stepping into glory where his Savior's praises would never cease.

Praising the Lord. Blessing His holy name.

It is how we *encourage ourselves in the Lord.*

Endnotes

[1] In light of the events of 1 Samuel 27:8-9, it would seem the Amalekites would have enacted revenge against David. When they kidnapped the women and children instead of killing them it most likely had the intention of selling them as slaves.

[2] Harris, R. L., Archer, G. L., Jr., & Waltke, B. K. (Eds.). (1999). Theological Wordbook of the Old Testament (electronic ed., pp. 778–779). Chicago: Moody Press.

[3] http://www.statisticbrain.com/stress-statistics/

[4] http://www.intothyword.org/apps/articles/?articleid=36562

[5] Baker, W., & Carpenter, E. E. (2003). The complete word study dictionary: Old Testament (p. 326). Chattanooga, TN: AMG Publishers.

[6] Faro, I. S. (2014). Strength. D. Mangum, D. R. Brown, R. Klippenstein, & R. Hurst (Eds.), Lexham Theological Wordbook. Bellingham, WA: Lexham Press.

[7] Weber, C. P. (1999). 636 חָזַק. R. L. Harris, G. L. Archer Jr., & B. K. Waltke (Eds.), Theological Wordbook of the Old Testament (electronic ed., p. 276). Chicago: Moody Press.

[8] http://www.chron.com/news/houston-texas/houston/article/Osteen-tour-tickets-are-a-hot-item-5531326.php

[9] Davis, D. R. (2000). 1 Samuel: Looking on the Heart (pp. 312–315). Scotland: Christian Focus Publications.

[10] The ephod worn by the high priest consisted of a sleeveless garment of fine twined lined decorated with gold and blue, purple, and scarlet material, to which two shoulder pieces were attached and around which fitted a belt...The ephod is at times clearly linked with eliciting an oracle from God...Most likely the ephod contained a pocket for the Urim and Thummim which were used for divination. (From: Myers, A. C. (1987). In The Eerdmans Bible dictionary (p. 342). Grand Rapids, MI: Eerdmans.)

[11] The phrase "Will of God" is found twenty three times in the New Testament. It is used to describe someone who is already living for the Will of God or to describe the choices of one seeking to live for the Will of God.

[12] http://www.robertjmorgan.com/hymn-stories/in-times-like-these/

[13] Smith, Alfred B. (1981). Al Smith's Treasury of Hymn Histories. Heritage Shoppe Distributing Company.

¹⁴ It is important to note that David's inspiration for the Psalms is far different from human inspiration that leads to the writing of music. Some singers and arrangers have claimed that the inspiration they received when writing a popular song is that same as Bible inspiration. This thinking is a sinful error. (See Revelation 22:18-19).

¹⁵ The Greek version of the Old Testament, the Septuagint, attributed a total of 86 Psalms to David.

¹⁶ Psalms 34; 52; 54; 56; 57; 63; 142

¹⁷ Wilson, J. L., & Russell, R. (2015). Burning His House down to Kill a Spider. In E. Ritzema (Ed.), 300 Illustrations for Preachers. Bellingham, WA: Lexham Press

¹⁸ The Hebrew root of the word used for man describes one who is weak, sick, and insignificant. It is a word used to show human frailty. (Theological Wordbook of the Old Testament)

¹⁹ VanGemeren, W. A. (1991). Psalms. In F. E. Gaebelein (Ed.), *The Expositor's Bible Commentary: Psalms, Proverbs, Ecclesiastes, Song of Songs* (Vol. 5, p. 398). Grand Rapids, MI: Zondervan Publishing House.

²⁰ Hamme, J. T. (2014). Salvation. D. Mangum, D. R. Brown, R. Klippenstein, & R. Hurst (Eds.), *Lexham Theological Wordbook*. Bellingham, WA: Lexham Press.

²¹ Wolf, H. (1999). R. L. Harris, G. L. Archer Jr., & B. K. Waltke (Eds.), *Theological Wordbook of the Old Testament* (electronic ed., p. 25). Chicago: Moody Press.

²² Oswalt, J. N. (1999). 233 בָּטַח. R. L. Harris, G. L. Archer Jr., & B. K. Waltke (Eds.), *Theological Wordbook of the Old Testament* (electronic ed., p. 101). Chicago: Moody Press.

²³ Phillips, John. Exploring Psalms: The John Phillips Commentary Series. Kregel Publications. Olive Tree Edition.

²⁴ Alexander, J. A. (1864). The Psalms Translated and Explained (p. 251). Edinburgh: Andrew Elliot; James Thin.

²⁵ The Hebrew words for wanderings and tears in verse 9 are in the singular. Every single wandering and every single tear was noted.

²⁶ Smith, Alfred B. (1981). Al Smith's Treasury of Hymn Histories. Heritage Shoppe Distributing Company.

²⁷ Graeff, Frank E. (1901). *Does Jesus Care?*

[28] Smith, S., & Cornwall, J. (1998). In The exhaustive dictionary of Bible names (p. 148). North Brunswick, NJ: Bridge-Logos.

[29] The title of the Psalm identifies the name of the king of Gath as Abimelech. 1 Samuel 21 uses the name Achish. One guess is that Achish was the natural name for the king, while Abimelech may have been an official title for the king (much like Pharaoh was an official title for Egyptian monarchs).

[30] Baker, W., & Carpenter, E. E. (2003). *The complete word study dictionary: Old Testament* (p. 714). Chattanooga, TN: AMG Publishers.

[31] Galaxie Software. (2002). 10,000 Sermon Illustrations. Biblical Studies Press.

[32] Hoffner, H. A., Jr. (2015). *1 & 2 Samuel*. (H. W. House & W. Barrick, Eds.) (1 Sa 21:8). Bellingham, WA: Lexham Press.

[33] Major Contributors and Editors. (2012, 2013, 2014, 2015). Doeg. In J. D. Barry, D. Bomar, D. R. Brown, R. Klippenstein, D. Mangum, C. Sinclair Wolcott, … W. Widder (Eds.), *The Lexham Bible Dictionary*. Bellingham, WA: Lexham Press.

[34] Coppes, L. J. (1999). 499 הָלַל. R. L. Harris, G. L. Archer Jr., & B. K. Waltke (Eds.), *Theological Wordbook of the Old Testament* (electronic ed., p. 217). Chicago: Moody Press.

[35] Spurgeon, Charles (2012-01-17). The Treasury of David: The Complete Seven Volumes (Kindle Locations 29555-29558). Kindle Edition.

[36] http://thefederalist.com/2015/09/29/a-quick-and-easy-guide-to-the-planned-parenthood-videos/

[37] https://www.lifesitenews.com/news/house-passes-1.1-trillion-spending-bill-that-fully-funds-planned-parenthood

[38] Smith, Alfred B. (1981). *Al Smith's Treasury of Hymn Histories*. (P. 63). Greenville, SC: Better Music Publications

[39] Wilson, G. H. (2002). *Psalms* (Vol. 1, p. 788). Grand Rapids, MI: Zondervan.

[40] Smith, Alfred B. (1981). Al Smith's Treasury of Hymn Histories. Heritage Shoppe Distributing Company.

[41] Scriven, Joseph. 1855. *What a Friend We Have In Jesus*. Public Domain

[42] Phillips, John. Exploring Psalms: The John Phillips Commentary Series. Kregel Publications. Olive Tree Edition.

[43] English Stand Version. Similar translation errors are found in the Revised Stand Version; The Good News Bible; The New International Version

[44] VanGemeren, W. A. (1991). Psalms. In F. E. Gaebelein (Ed.), *The Expositor's Bible Commentary: Psalms, Proverbs, Ecclesiastes, Song of Songs* (Vol. 5, p. 391). Grand Rapids, MI: Zondervan Publishing House.

[45] There is a debate as to whether David was in the Cave Adullum or the Cave of Engedi when he penned Psalm 57. I believe he is in the cave of Engedi because the title says he was fleeing "from Saul." In the Cave of Adullum he was fleeing from Achish.

[46] Spurgeon, Charles (2012-01-17). The Treasury of David: The Complete Seven Volumes (Kindle Locations 1754-1758). Kindle Edition.

[47] Cushing, William. 1896. *Under His Wings.* Public Domain

[48] Spurgeon, C. H. (1879). Among Lions. In *The Metropolitan Tabernacle Pulpit Sermons* (Vol. 25, p. 543). London: Passmore & Alabaster.

[49] Lookadoo, J. (2014). Body. D. Mangum, D. R. Brown, R. Klippenstein, & R. Hurst (Eds.), Lexham Theological Wordbook. Bellingham, WA: Lexham Press.

[50] Baker, W., & Carpenter, E. E. (2003). The complete word study dictionary: Old Testament (p. 499). Chattanooga, TN: AMG Publishers.

[51] Osbeck, K. W. (1996). Amazing grace: 366 inspiring hymn stories for daily devotions (p. 348). Grand Rapids, MI: Kregel Publications.

[52] Baker, W., & Carpenter, E. E. (2003). The complete word study dictionary: Old Testament (p. 816). Chattanooga, TN: AMG Publishers.

[53] Major Contributors and Editors. (2012, 2013, 2014, 2015). Al-Taschith. In J. D. Barry, D. Bomar, D. R. Brown, R. Klippenstein, D. Mangum, C. Sinclair Wolcott, … W. Widder (Eds.), The Lexham Bible Dictionary. Bellingham, WA: Lexham Press.

[54] Baker, W., & Carpenter, E. E. (2003). *The complete word study dictionary: Old Testament* (p. 1144). Chattanooga, TN: AMG Publishers.

[55] Hope, N. V. (1992). Studd, Charles Thomas. In J. D. Douglas & P. W. Comfort (Eds.), *Who's Who in Christian history* (p. 645). Wheaton, IL: Tyndale House.

[56] http://hockleys.org/2009/05/quote-only-one-life-twill-soon-be-past-poem/

[57] https://en.wikipedia.org/wiki/Aristides

58 Boice, J. M. (2005). Psalms 1–41: An Expositional Commentary (p. 38). Grand Rapids, MI: Baker Books.

59 Baker, W., & Carpenter, E. E. (2003). The complete word study dictionary: Old Testament (pp. 705–706). Chattanooga, TN: AMG Publishers.

60 VanGemeren, W. A. (1991). Psalms. In F. E. Gaebelein (Ed.), *The Expositor's Bible Commentary: Psalms, Proverbs, Ecclesiastes, Song of Songs* (Vol. 5, p. 82). Grand Rapids, MI: Zondervan Publishing House.

61 Spurgeon, Charles (2012-01-17). The Treasury of David: The Complete Seven Volumes (Kindle Locations 2170-2171) Kindle Edition

62 Wilson, G. H. (2002). Psalms (Vol. 1, p. 157). Grand Rapids, MI: Zondervan.

63 Mounce, William D. (2006). Mounce's Complete Expository Dictionary of Old and New Testament Words. Grand Rapids, MI: Zondervan

64 Tovey, Herbert G. (1914). *Give Me a Passion for Souls.*

65 https://en.wikipedia.org/wiki/William_Palmer_(murderer)

66 Spurgeon, C. H. (1856). The New Park Street Pulpit Sermons (Vol. 2, p. 257). London: Passmore & Alabaster.

67 Tate, M. E. (1998). Psalms 51–100 (Vol. 20, pp. 27–28). Dallas: Word, Incorporated.

68 Baker, W., & Carpenter, E. E. (2003). The complete word study dictionary: Old Testament (pp. 364–365). Chattanooga, TN: AMG Publishers.

69 Baker, W., & Carpenter, E. E. (2003). The complete word study dictionary: Old Testament (p. 927). Chattanooga, TN: AMG Publishers.

70 DiFransico, L. (2014). Guilt. D. Mangum, D. R. Brown, R. Klippenstein, & R. Hurst (Eds.), Lexham Theological Wordbook. Bellingham, WA: Lexham Press.

71 Livingston, G. H. (1999). 638 חָטָא. R. L. Harris, G. L. Archer Jr., & B. K. Waltke (Eds.), Theological Wordbook of the Old Testament (electronic ed., p. 277). Chicago: Moody Press.

72 Hamme, J. T. (2014). Salvation. D. Mangum, D. R. Brown, R. Klippenstein, & R. Hurst (Eds.), Lexham Theological Wordbook. Bellingham, WA: Lexham Press.

73 Baker, W., & Carpenter, E. E. (2003). The complete word study dictionary: Old Testament (p. 593). Chattanooga, TN: AMG Publishers.

[74] Osbeck, K. W. (1996). Amazing grace: 366 inspiring hymn stories for daily devotions (p. 194). Grand Rapids, MI: Kregel Publications.

[75] Spurgeon, Charles (2012-01-17). The Treasury of David: The Complete Seven Volumes (Kindle Locations 1767-1773). Kindle Edition.

[76] Wilson, G. H. (2002). *Psalms* (Vol. 1, p. 129). Grand Rapids, MI: Zondervan.

[77] Liberal scholars often attack the authenticity of the superscripts in Psalms. They claim (as they do with many passages of the Bible) that they were added at a later time. But there is no evidence supporting such a theory. They are found in the most ancients copies of Scripture, and there is no reason to doubt them.

[78] 1 Kings 22:4; Isaiah 50:6; Lamentations 3:30; Micah 5:1

[79] Numbers 10:35; Psalms 3:8; 7:6; 9:19; 10:12; 17:13; 35:2; 44:26; 74:22; 82:8; 132:8; Jeremiah 2:27; 2 Chronicles 6:41

[80] Nutter, C. S., & Tillett, W. F. (1911). *The Hymns and Hymn Writers of the Church: An Annotated Edition of the Methodist Hymnal* (Vol. 1, p. 411). New York; Cincinnati; Nashville: Eaton & Mains; Jennings & Graham; Smith & Lamar.

[81] http://ministry127.com/resources/illustration/faith-to-sleep

[82] Phillips, John. Exploring Psalms: The John Phillips Commentary Series. Kregel Publications. Olive Tree Edition.

[83] "Marrow and fatness" represent the finest of foods. It is the "designation of a feast prepared from well-fed, noble beasts." It describes the contentment of a man who has just enjoyed the greatest of royal feasts. (Keil, C. F., & Delitzsch, F. (1996). *Commentary on the Old Testament* (Vol. 5, p. 424). Peabody, MA: Hendrickson.)

[84] Wilson, G. H. (2002). Psalms (Vol. 1, p. 890). Grand Rapids, MI: Zondervan.

[85] Morgan, Robert J. (2004). Then Sings My Soul (Book 2, p. 184). Nashville, TN: Thomas Nelson

[86] Smith, Alfred B. (1981). Al Smith's Treasury of Hymn Histories. Heritage Shoppe Distributing Company.

Aug. 22, 21

I cannot be silent - I
want to shout from a
roof top - Thank you Jesus
in the midst of this storm
Hurricane Henri - a greater
storm has been about
us, Spiritual, hard & long
battered. And yet at this
moment God in His mercy
And grace has his child
David standing again in the
Nursing Home - How the Lord
alone brought us here today
And many times before - Wind
howls, trees sway - debris all
around - Gods Word goes forth
I feel so Alive in His presence
PS. 51

Books By Paul Schwanke

Major Messages from Minor Prophets Series

Evangelist Paul Schwanke
www.preachthebible.com

Made in the USA
San Bernardino, CA
11 July 2018